T0171364

What if a passage from the Bible explaining how God designed church leadership applies to all organizations? As a student of the Bible and a consummate businessman, Walt Pilcher is in a good position to address the question. With an engaging style and clear writing, Walt examines the essence of the biblical model and builds an analogous model for all organizations. He draws on his own experiences to begin to test the model, demonstrating how filling all of the Ephesians 4:11 roles can greatly increase the effectiveness and efficiency of an organization. This model has great potential to supercharge productivity and bring fulfillment to each person in the leadership team. I hope this book inspires you to try the five-fold approach and report your experience to the author. This could be the start of a revolutionary movement in organizational leadership!

Dr. John E. Mulford
Director, Regent University Center for Entrepreneurship
Former Dean, Regent University Business School

The Five-fold Effect: Unlocking Power Leadership for Amazing Results in Your Organization is a fine book that will help any leader take his or her organization to the next level. Written in an engaging, conversational style, *The Five-fold Effect* blends humor, practical advice and foundational principles from which any leader will benefit. As author Walt Pilcher rightly notes, "This book is not only for business and church. It is for anyone, anywhere, of any age or gender, Christian or non-Christian, who works with other people."

Dr. Carlos Campo
President
Regent University
Making the Extraordinary our Standard

This is the first whole book I am aware of that specifically focuses on how the five-fold gifts of Ephesians 4:11 fit into the workplace. It is well-structured, well-thought out, well-researched, and well-written. With all modesty, as I read it, I realized that I could not have written it any better!

Dr. C. Peter Wagner
Vice President and Apostolic Ambassador
Global Spheres Inc., Colorado Mission

Walt Pilcher has written a fascinating book that looks at business from the paradigm of the five-fold offices of Ephesians 4: apostles, prophets, evangelists, pastors and teachers. By applying these office gifts to the marketplace he reveals an understanding of how the offices work together in the business arena to cause a company to be built faster and become a stronger, greater company. His practical illustrations and examples help one take the spiritual framework from which he is working and more easily understand the application in the business arena. Walt's activation exercises help solidify the understanding of how these biblical gifts/offices of the church have modern day applications for business. Walt's successful career as the president of a couple of Fortune 500 companies and his experience in church and non-profit Christian organizations make him exceptionally qualified for writing such a book as *The Five-fold Effect*. I highly recommend it.

Randy Clark
Founder and President
The Apostolic Network of Global Awakening

I am always impacted by successful real world executives and CEOs who embrace the power of God and the fullness of the book of Acts. Walt Pilcher is at the top of his game in this subject. He has the ability to dissect a ministry or a business with the speed of a javelin and the accuracy of a jeweler's eye. As we sort out the emerging role of believers in the 7M arenas (seven mountains), I can't wait to see the impact *The Five-fold Effect* will have on the world.

Dr. Lance Wallnau
International speaker on the Seven Mountains of Influence and
President of Lance Learning Group

God has clearly expressed in the scriptures the way to release His people into maximum creativity and productivity. Walt has captured for the business world this explosive revelation that is emerging in the church. It is about recognizing and releasing the people resources and gifts that can bring success to any organization. Walt brings a very special perspective to this transformational opportunity. He has proven success in the business world and a depth of insight into God ordained ways. I recommend this book as unique in these uncertain days as a sure biblical foundation for growth.

Rodney Odom
Senior Leader
Grace Church, High Point, North Carolina

The Five-fold Effect provides a much-needed bridge between the Kingdom of God, the seven mountains of culture, and the church of Jesus. The fact that this book had to be written at all tells us something about the state of the church and that some unfortunately have not yet learned or understood that the way we are to be salt and light, the yeast hidden in the loaf, and the pearl of great price to those around us and in our spheres of influence, is through the five-fold expression of Jesus' nature and spiritual DNA through you and me.

The Kingdom of God is within us, according to Luke 17:21, and likewise, the five-fold is within us as well according to the good pleasure and free gift of Jesus. That one expression of the five-fold is in the church does not preclude or prevent its expression in the broader society and culture, including the marketplace and government. In fact, that is one of its primary purposes, and in the Hebraic setting and context of the titular Scripture, and Pauline intent of Ephesians 4:11, there is integration rather than separation between these spheres. Ephesians 4:11–16 is a mandate for a self-replicating and self-perpetuating model for multiplication, manifestation and miracles, wherever it shows up, and in whatever form it takes.

Every follower of Jesus is gifted in some measure, and as we learn to think of church more in terms of people and relationships rather than buildings and denominations, and as we shift our thinking and perspective from a local church or denominational level to the Kingdom of God globally, the principles presented in *The Five-fold Effect* will become more widely accepted and practiced in the other six mountains.

Walt Pilcher is to be commended for discerning and stewarding this revelation, and sharing it with the rest of us—the body and bride of Christ. I recommend this book and its author, and encourage you to read and apply this book and its wisdom in your own life, family, church, business, agency, organization, city, nation, and/or sphere of influence.

Dr. Bruce Cook
President, KEYS Network, VentureAdvisers, Inc.,
Kingdom House Publishing
Author, *Partnering with the Prophetic* and *Aligning with the Apostolic*

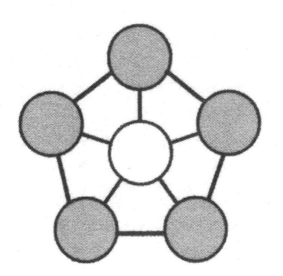

THE
FIVE-FOLD
EFFECT

Unlocking Power Leadership
for Amazing Results in
Your Organization

WALT PILCHER

WESTBOW
PRESS
A DIVISION OF THOMAS NELSON

WestBow Press books may be ordered through booksellers or by contacting:

WestBow Press
A Division of Thomas Nelson
1663 Liberty Drive
Bloomington, IN 47403
www.westbowpress.com
1-(866) 928-1240

ISBN: 978-1-4497-9005-9 (sc)
ISBN: 978-1-4497-9006-6 (hc)
ISBN: 978-1-4497-9004-2 (e)

Library of Congress Control Number: 2013905963

Printed in the United States of America.
WestBow Press rev. date: 04/18/13

TABLE OF CONTENTS

DEDICATION

To my father, Major General Milton A. Pilcher, USAR (Ret), who by his example nurtured my inherent leadership gifts and who saw to it that I had every opportunity to become equipped to use them effectively. With quiet faith, discipline and determination, my father models leadership for his family and the church he has served for many years, as well as for the military commands and civil service agencies he has served during his distinguished career as an outstanding member of "The Greatest Generation." Thanks, Dad.

ACKNOWLEDGEMENTS

In addition to Dr. Mark Virkler, who graciously wrote the Foreword, and all those who kindly provided endorsements, I want to thank my "first readers" who volunteered their time and talent to read and provide feedback even before they knew what they were getting into, and surprisingly more so after they found out. You know who you are, but first and foremost, and truly more than a "first reader," is my wife, Carol Pilcher, who read the earliest drafts more than once and made foundational suggestions that helped shape the structure of the book and ensured its positive and optimistic tone.

I am grateful to the Grace Church 411 Group for being the patient audience for my "trial balloon" presentation of the key ideas in the book and to the Tuesday Forum prayer group for their unwavering support and encouragement as I worked on it. Special thanks also to Randy Clark, Bo Kenan, Jon Koch, Theresa Koch, John Mullen, Rodney Odom, Tom O'Shea, Dick Robinson, and Matt Rose for your critical comments, suggestions and encouragement throughout the process. Free copies for all of you!

I thank the Holy Spirit for the initial and continuing vision for the book, and I give glory to God for what I pray will be its significant impact on the world.

"They *first* got the right people on the bus (and the wrong people off the bus) and *then* figured out where to drive it."

— Jim Collins in *Good to Great*
HarperCollins Publishers, Inc.

If you can't do that, then get the people who are on your bus to sit where they will do the most good while you help them to become the right people.

— Walt Pilcher

THE
FIVE-FOLD
EFFECT

FOREWORD

This book, *The Five-fold Effect: Unlocking Power Leadership for Amazing Results in Your Organization,* is of outstanding value to any leader who is seeking to grow his business or church by incorporating the divine wisdom that comes from a properly functioning five-fold team of multi-gifted individuals. To understand this five-fold team leadership concept, and then to have a working manual which helps you integrate it into the hearts of your leaders, is a priceless gem. This book will help many Kingdom-minded businesses and churches grow into the destiny God has for them.

There is only one list of gifts in the New Testament that comes with a promise attached to it: the list in Ephesians 4:11 of apostle, prophet, evangelist, pastor and teacher. The promise is that the proper functioning of such a team of individuals causes one to come to maturity (Ephesians 4:13). That sets this specific list apart from all other lists of gifts in the New Testament. I want to come to maturity. I want my business to come to maturity. I want my church to come to maturity. So Ephesians 4:11–16 tells me that this will happen if the above five heart motivations are present in the team of consultants which are helping the business or ministry make wise decisions.

So what are these five heart motivations? Can I name them? Can I recognize them in the people that surround me? Is there a way I can ensure they are all present in helping my church or business grow and make wise, Spirit-led decisions? How do I make certain all five voices are heard, honored, and integrated into the final solution to the issue we are exploring? You will discover answers to all these questions plus much more in this book, *The Five-fold Effect: Unlocking Power Leadership for Amazing Results in Your Organization.*

Walt, thank you for creating this book and making it available to those who are pressing forward in a Kingdom mentality. Thank you for helping strip away the false dichotomy between sacred and secular, and showing us that God's divine principles work just as well in the business arena as they do in the church. We have chosen to use this outstanding book at Christian Leadership University in our course "Building Dynamic Teams." It will be a blessing to our students as it was to me.

Mark Virkler
President, Christian Leadership University

INTRODUCTION

Here's an idea: What if there is a way to turn your business or organization into the most effective, powerful and successful organization of its kind, ever?

What if God has a plan for how things should operate in the marketplace and you can tap into it? What if the world already uses a poor imitation of this plan, having forgotten where it came from? What if we, and by "we" I mean "you," apply the original plan in your church and to your life in the marketplace?

What if I stop asking these questions and start explaining how God's plan, when applied with intentionality and understanding, can transform not only your organization, but also the world?

WHAT'S THE PLAN?

This seemingly revolutionary plan is based on the five-fold ministry gifts found in Ephesians 4:11–16.

11 And He Himself gave some to be apostles, some prophets, some evangelists, and some pastors and teachers, [12] for the equipping of the saints for the work of ministry, for the edifying of the body of Christ, [13] till we all come to

the unity of the faith and of the knowledge of the Son of God, to a perfect man, to the measure of the stature of the fullness of Christ;

[14] that we should no longer be children, tossed to and fro and carried about with every wind of doctrine, by the trickery of men, in the cunning craftiness of deceitful plotting, [15] but, speaking the truth in love, may grow up in all things into Him who is the head—Christ— [16] from whom the whole body, joined and knit together by what every joint supplies, according to the effective working by which every part does its share, causes growth of the body for the edifying of itself in love (NKJV).

We know this passage as God's model for how the church is to function. Within it are the keys to the most effective leadership, governance and organization of the church universal[1] and for individual churches. In a local church it looks like this:

A body led by elders representing each of the five-fold gifts and under the authority of a leader with apostolic gifting. These leaders train and equip others to operate in these five and other gifts in order to work together perfectly, by the power of the Holy Spirit, so that the church accomplishes its mission.

Not only are the original *offices* of apostle and prophet in operation today, but also the apostolic and prophetic *gifts* and *functions* are very much in operation, along with those of evangelist, pastor and teacher.

---

1   I have chosen not to capitalize "church" unless it is in a title or caption, capitalized in a quotation, a proper name, or part of the name of a specific church, such as the Methodist Church as a denomination or Grace Church of High Point, NC, or begins a sentence. To capitalize it otherwise would be to characterize the church as some kind of formal institution or organization, which it is not. The church is the 2.2 billion individual believers who make up what the Bible calls "the body of Christ" (especially 1 Corinthians 12:27 and Ephesians 4:12).

We know this for many reasons, but for starters we have only to look at the language that says, "till we all come to the unity of the faith and of the knowledge of the Son of God, to a perfect man, to the measure of the stature of the fullness of Christ" and "that we . . . may grow up in all things into Him who is the head—Christ." Since this clearly hasn't happened fully yet, there is good reason to believe He hasn't removed the gifts He provided to help bring it about.

All of these gifts, when exercised wisely together, greatly and supernaturally add to the ability of a church body to realize the fulfillment of God's purposes for people's lives and His purposes for that body. This is what I call "The Five-fold Effect."

Figure I–1 is a simple graphic representation of the five-fold ministry model and the close relationships between each of its five elements and the church body or congregation. You will see this diagram again in Chapter 4 with variations of it presented and explained throughout the book as visual aids to the understanding of the concepts being discussed. For now, just get familiar with its overall look and shape, and keep it in mind as an aid in thinking about five-fold leadership. You'll notice I've also used it as an icon on the first page of each chapter of the book.

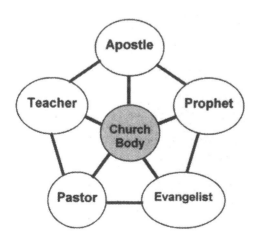

Figure I–1: Five-Fold Ministry Gifts for the Church

But it's not just for the church.

The five-fold ministry plan of leadership was given to the church, but it is intended for the marketplace as much as it is for the church. That means it is for our everyday lives, activities and businesses. You and I have an opportunity today to apply it in our own spheres of influence and thereby enjoy The Five-fold Effect in our lives. Furthermore, I believe this has been God's plan all along, from the Beginning.

That's what this book is about. What The Five-fold Effect is, how it works, and how to apply its principles to your life and your business, which is part of your marketplace ministry.

Is God in the Marketplace?

Since the Garden of Eden

Can we really find God in the marketplace? Does He want to be there? Shouldn't religion and business be kept separate? The answers are Yes, Yes, and No.

God has been "in the marketplace" since the Garden of Eden. He gave Adam and Eve dominion over the earth (Genesis 1:28). That meant they had the job of cultivating and developing it. God's plan was for the Garden of Eden eventually to encompass the whole earth and be a divinely perfect, peaceful dwelling place for all mankind, with God dwelling with us.

Sure, God provided everything for Adam and Eve at first. All they had to do was eat the low hanging fruit, just like a baby who knows nothing and contributes nothing but gets all its needs met because its parents love it. But they (we) were expected to grow and mature, and He was teaching them about the responsibilities they would eventually bear. Those were easy burdens with a light yoke, but still it was work for them to do, work He had prepared ahead of time, literally, that is, before time began (Ephesians 2:10).

It was their mission[2] in life, their *business,* to develop commerce (agriculture, manufacturing, trading, etc.), and from it to provide for themselves and their family. Although He *gave* them dominion over the earth, they still had to actually *take* it. Dominion is an action word, not just a state of being.

It didn't work out because they didn't trust God. However, the rest of the Bible is the story of God's plan to restore us to that place! *This idea is central to why we need to learn to apply the leadership principles of the five- fold ministry to the marketplace.*

THE THESIS:
WORLD-CHANGING IMPLICATIONS

Here is why understanding and applying the five-fold ministry is so important and could change the world. Consider these two levels of application and effectiveness:

Level 1

Teams of leaders with complementary gift sets corresponding to the five-fold gifts of the Spirit (as well as the motivational gifts of Romans 12:3–8[3]) will create organizations that are more successful than those not led in that way because

---

2   From the Latin word, *mittere,* meaning "to send." It is the root of such words as "commission," "missionary," "missile," and even "committee." "Apostle" means "the sent one," from the Greek *apostellein,* meaning "to send away." So if you find yourself in an apostolic role, consider yourself a missile from God. Just don't blow up when things don't go smoothly unless you can shower everyone with the shrapnel of love. (Hey, wouldn't "The Shrapnel of Love" make a great rock song?)

3   From Romans 12:3–8: Perceiving, serving, teaching, encouraging, giving, ruling, and mercy.

working together in concert and alignment is more efficient than working alone or at cross purposes.[4]

Level 2
Organizations that not only employ the paradigm above, but also are led by people who have a relationship with Jesus and an indwelling of the Holy Spirit, combined with an understanding of how to be led by Him in the exercise of their Holy Spirit-given gifts, will operate in much more power and therefore enjoy much more effectiveness and success than those that do not.

Both levels are desirable, but imagine how much better Level 2 can be when you are receiving supernatural help! Furthermore, the world is changing at an accelerating rate. We will need more than natural agility to keep up. Church and marketplace organizations will need supernatural help not only to keep up, but also to anticipate and prepare for the future as well as to be change-makers themselves. They will need The Five-fold Effect.

WHY THIS BOOK?

The five-fold ministry gifts originated with and for the church. The church should use them, of course, but also the church should teach and apply them in the marketplace. Instead, often we try to apply the world's poor imitation of the real thing to the church. We've got it backwards!

Learning to employ the five-fold plan in any organization would be to ignite a keg of spiritual dynamite that would allow the Holy Spirit to work mightily in its success. Yet we rarely see it recognized outside of some church and para-church organizations,

---

4   "In the multitude of counselors there is safety" (Prov. 11:14) and "...a threefold cord is not easily broken" (Eccl. 4:12)

and even those rarely seem to approach it in a disciplined way. This is an unfulfilled Kingdom need whose time has come, and it is why I've written this book.

The idea that "our work is our ministry" is not a novel one anymore, thanks to the Holy Spirit and many good authors, pastors and teachers. Likewise our play, our family life, and anything else we do, is a ministry, especially if it involves serving others in any way. In the New Testament the Greek word *diakonia* is translated as "ministry" about half the time and "service" about half the time.[5] In fact, the word "minister" is the same word in Latin and means "servant." Therefore, service is ministry, and *vice versa*. That you are called to be a marketplace minister of some kind is now a given, sort of like the price of admission or the prerequisite to advancing to the next level of a video game.

However, this is not another book on how to do marketplace ministry or operate a "Kingdom business."[6] There are already many good books about that. It's pretty well accepted by now that God wants us to tear down the walls between the churches and the community and take our Christian witness to the marketplace where we live and work six days a week when we're not in church. As a Christian you are already a witness for the Kingdom wherever you go, whether you know it or not. We all can use instruction on how to be good witnesses, and I applaud the teaching that is

---

5   From C. Peter Wagner, *The Church in the Workplace*, Regal Books, Ventura, CA, 2006, pp. 108–109.

6   "Kingdom business" connotes a business that is not only run by biblical principles, but also has an agenda, or at least a mind-set, involving the use of the business for the furtherance of God's purposes on Earth, typically involving improving the quality of life for owners, employees, customers and all others who are touched by it, ideally leading ultimately to Christian evangelism. Google "Kingdom business" to find many sites and organizations dedicated to furthering this concept. One with which I have some familiarity is the Regent University Center for Entrepreneurship, under the direction of Dr. John Mulford (www.regententrepreneur.org/kingdom-business).

available. *But this book goes far beyond that by presenting a paradigm for organizational transformation that has been overlooked for centuries, yet is as close as our fingertips and is easy to apply in everyday life and work. It's the next level, and maybe the ultimate one.*[7]

Here's a surprise: You don't have to be a Christian to benefit from the concepts presented here. Although this book is full of biblical references and honors God the Father, Jesus Christ His Son, and the Holy Spirit, the principles work whether you believe in their source or not. They are like laws of nature. There is no refuting them. They just work, every time, all the time. Although there is some churchy talk in this book, don't let it get in your way. Just grin and bear it as you glean and benefit from the truths it reveals. If nothing else, you will learn to apply the Romans 12:3–8 "motivational gifts" of perceiving, serving, teaching, encouraging, giving, ruling, and mercy, which are pretty well accepted in the secular world, and at the very least you can count yourself among those enjoying the fruit of effectiveness Level 1.

But, "What if?" What if it's true? Wouldn't it be great to go to Level 2, to operate in real supernatural power from the Holy Spirit and see results you've only dreamed of until now? Jesus said, "I am come that they might have life, and that they might have it more abundantly" (John 10:10, KJV). He also said, "'For I know the plans I have for you,' declares the Lord, 'plans to prosper you and not to harm you, plans to give you hope and a future'" (Jeremiah 29:11). Realize that God loves everyone and wants everyone to succeed. Use these principles, and in so doing get to know the One

---

7   Please excuse the hubris, but obviously I'm excited about this. However, I don't presume any revelation from God, however dramatic, is the ultimate one until Jesus returns. Too many people and denominations have camped out around a major revelation, refusing to budge from it while the rest of the church has moved on. On the other hand, Ephesians 4:11–16 is the only place in the Bible where God describes His plan for organizational leadership, so maybe it's not a stretch to call it "ultimate." Additional revelation will come in terms of how we apply the plan.

who established them. He wants a relationship with you through which to bring you joy, peace, and success not only in business but also in every area of your life.

So, if you're not a Christian, read on anyway and you will be blessed. No, it won't "zap!" you into becoming a Christian. Only you can decide to do that. But I hope you will.

As you can see, at the end of the day this is actually an evangelistic book. I hope to intrigue non-Christians by the theory and potential success of wise application of five-fold ministry leadership. More than that, however, as you and your organization succeed in your own real world application, people will be drawn to you and will ask you how you did it. That's an invitation to tell them exactly what you have been up to. Your results will be a compelling witness to the power of the Holy Spirit and the glory of God.

What's in the Book?

I will begin by telling a story about the origins of this book, how it started for me. Then I will outline the biblical basis for the contention that the five-fold leadership plan has been in existence both for the church *and* for the marketplace since the beginning of Man's life on Earth. I'll follow that with what it looks like in church, what each of the five-fold gifts is and how they cooperate in work and ministry, and how to determine which gifts you have as well as the gifts of others around you. The largest section of the book will be devoted to the practical aspects of applying the five-fold principles to your marketplace activities, i.e., your business or other organization.

Who Should Read this Book?

When people ask, "Is this a business book or a church book?"

my answer is, it's both and more. True, *The Five-fold Effect* emphasizes how five-fold ministry principles can be applied in business settings. That's because most readers can relate to business since most now are or have been connected with business in one way or another in their lives, as owners, managers or employees of businesses of all shapes and sizes. Economic development, the free enterprise system, and the creation of jobs and a nation's wealth are very much on my mind, and the principles in the book can greatly impact that realm, or that "mountain of influence."[8] Even with that bias, however, all of the other six mountains of influence are most definitely included. Five-fold leadership applies to government, family, media, arts and entertainment, education, and to the church of course, as well as to business and commerce. If you think about it, they are all tied together.

Therefore, this book is not only for business and church. It is for anyone, anywhere, of any age or gender, Christian or non-Christian, who works with other people.

A LITTLE HOUSEKEEPING

In the book I refer to the five-fold "thing" variously as gifts, ministry, leadership, a model, a plan, a paradigm or principles. The Bible doesn't say what to call it, but we know it started out as consultative "gifts" He provided as leadership authority and

---

8   In 1975 Bill Bright, founder of Campus Crusade and Loren Cunningham, founder of Youth With A Mission, discovered that God had simultaneously given each of them a message for the other: "The culture is shaped by seven mind-molders or mountains in society." These have come to be known as "The Seven Mountains of Influence" (business, government, arts and entertainment, media, family, education, and religion) and have been written about and preached extensively by such proponents as Dr. Lance Wallnau, Dr. C. Peter Wagner, and Os Hillman. The graduate school curriculum of Regent University is centered on these culture changing areas.

resources for church governance and operation. Since I'm describing how five-fold is for both church *and* secular organizational leadership and governance, I'll use it sometimes as a noun and sometimes as an adjective modifying the other noun terms, and I'll choose those according to context.

I have included "Activation Exercises" at the ends of the chapters to help you incorporate the concepts not only into your mind but also into your spirit. In effect, you will begin actually practicing some of the ideas presented as each chapter builds to the next. I hope you will do the exercises. I've tried to make them interesting and practical.

Please don't even think about skipping over to the practical application sections of the book to avoid reading the background material, even if you already accept the thesis. You will miss a lot of the "why and how" that is needed to help you internalize the new paradigm, the new way of thinking about organizational leadership.

There will also be some surprises and some fun. I have determined not to write a dry book about biblical principles, so I've broken a few rules in order to provide what I hope is an engaging and sometimes entertaining practical guide to a new paradigm.

By the end of the process, I hope you will have the new paradigm firmly fixed in your mind and spirit and will be ready to start applying it in your life and in the lives of others in the spheres of influence and responsibility God has called you to. Your organizations, your endeavors, and your life can be supernaturally productive and effective. They will be a blessing to all those who come in contact with them.

ONE MORE THING

Before we get started, I want you to read and meditate on Romans 12. It is reprinted in Appendix A for your convenience.

Flip back there now. I believe it expresses the heart attitude we must have before embarking on any endeavor that involves working with other people. As you meditate on it and let it sink into your spirit, you will be preparing yourself to receive and act successfully upon the revelations of this book. We will look at it again at the end of the book.

Okay, now get ready to unlock and enjoy The Five-fold Effect!

CHAPTER 1

A VISION TOO SMALL

THE GENESIS OF THIS BOOK

One weekend in 2003 while I was at Regent University in Virginia Beach, Virginia, for a meeting of the Board of Trustees, Dr. John Mulford, the dean of the Graduate School of Business at that time, lent me his copy of *Good to Great* by Jim Collins. *Good to Great* was the "hot" business book of the day. Dr. Mulford had enjoyed it and thought I would too. He was right. I practically devoured it, starting it in his office and reading during breaks from Board meeting activities and at night in my hotel room. I finished it before the weekend was over.

In addition to being well-written and engaging, what struck me about the book were the characteristics of the chief executive officers of 11 companies the author singled out as having made the leap to greatness. They had something very interesting in common.

At about that same time, I was also involved in long-range planning as an elder in a growing Presbyterian church in my city of Greensboro, North Carolina. This involved the usual drafting of vision and mission statements, core values, strategies and objectives, organizational plans, and so forth. Being a businessman, I was inclined to apply business planning principles to running our church. Church management needs business management expertise, right? And after all, what do churches know of such things?

Therefore, the structure of our elders' long-range planning retreat agenda and the long-range plan itself looked like it could have been taken from that of any large company. And indeed it was. I had enjoyed a long career with Sara Lee Corporation, one of the best companies in the world at strategic planning. For the church plan, we basically just substituted churchy words for business words and referenced Scripture a lot.

I'm not saying this was bad. It was an effective approach, not only because it brought discipline to the planning process, but also because it forced us to pause and take stock of all the functions of the church, their purposes, and what it took to lead them well.

Enter Ephesians 4

But there was something nagging at me, a catch in my spirit that made me feel like maybe we were missing something. Having attended a "prophetic conference" at Grace Church in High Point, North Carolina, put on by a team led by Peter Butt from Southampton, England, I had become interested in the subject of "the prophetic" and had begun reading more about it. One especially interesting book was *A Divine Confrontation: Birth Pangs of the New Church* by Graham Cooke who is a highly respected author and international speaker. In it, he talks about the consultative roles of each of the five-fold ministry offices from Ephesians 4:11–16.

Like many of us, I had read that passage a thousand times, where it says, "It was he who gave some to be apostles, some to be prophets, some to be evangelists, and some to be pastors and teachers, to prepare God's people for works of service, so that the body of Christ may be built up" and so on. This passage sounded pretty foundational to me, but I had never heard any teaching on it. In our church we knew a lot about evangelism, we had some good teachers, and the head leader was the "senior pastor." However, apostles and prophets were rarely mentioned, and when they were they were dismissed as having been important in biblical times, but not today.

Why, then, would this passage be included in the Bible, the same book where Jesus says to His 11 faithful disciples, "All authority in heaven and on earth has been given to me. Therefore go and make disciples of all nations, baptizing them in the name of the Father and of the Son and of the Holy Spirit, and *teaching them to obey everything I have commanded you*. And surely I am with you always, *to the very end of the age*" (Matthew 28:18b–20, italics added).

I believe this is the point at which the disciples became apostles, "sent" to carry out this commission, needing only the indwelling of the Holy Spirit which occurred at Pentecost to empower them to do it well.[9] Because of the apostles' faithfulness and obedience we, too, have been made disciples, taught to obey the commands Jesus gave His disciples, doing so by the leading and power of the Holy Spirit.

What He "commanded you" (us) includes healing the sick, driving out demons, raising the dead, and "even greater things" (Matthew 10:7–8, Luke 9:1–2, Luke 10:9, John 14:12). As believers we know that Jesus' Spirit is in us. Therefore, we carry the authority He was given and that He gave to his disciples.

Unless Jesus was just kidding, then Jesus-in-us-and-with-us will

---

9   Actually, the first time the 11 are called apostles is earlier in Matthew 10:1–2 when Jesus "gave them authority" to go out on their first mission alone. Arguably, they did not fully step into that office until Jesus' Ascension. "Disciple" is from the Latin *discipulus*, which means "student." Quite a promotion from student to apostle!

continue to the end of the age, i.e., until He returns. Have we made disciples of all nations yet? Not by a long shot. Therefore, all of that power, those gifts He gave us, must still be for today. And if so, then that means, like the disciples who became apostles, we too must become "apostolic," or apostle-like, to carry out the mission that has been handed down to us. Those were my thoughts about it.

Blank Stares

It seemed to me that learning more about this would be important to the future of our church. However, when I suggested we study the subject and see if the Lord would tell us how to apply it, I got mostly blank stares. Nobody had a grid for it and, worse, it seemed to involve using the nine gifts of the Spirit from 1 Corinthians 12:8–10[10] which, except for the gift of faith, we had been taught were irrelevant at best, definitely "not for today," and even dangerous. Some of them might be "of the devil," and we certainly didn't want to "be deceived."

Nevertheless, Graham Cooke's book, and others, began to open me up to a better understanding of the five-fold ministry gifts and how they might operate in the church. Cooke explains the roles of each of the five gifts and how they are supposed to relate to each other for the purpose of "equipping the saints." I began to observe the characteristics displayed by people carrying these gifts. It was a great revelation, and it unexpectedly rang a bell as I read *Good to Great* that weekend at Regent University.

---

10 "To one there is given through the Spirit the message of wisdom, to another the message of knowledge by means of the same Spirit, to another faith by the same Spirit, to another gifts of healing by that one Spirit, to another miraculous powers, to another prophecy, to another distinguishing between spirits, to another speaking in different kinds of tongues, and to still another the interpretation of tongues."

THE LESSON OF GOOD TO GREAT

For *Good to Great*, Jim Collins studied 28 well-known companies, of which 11 stood out for having greatly outperformed their peer companies over a 15 year period. The key question was, "What did the 11 good-to-great companies share in common *that distinguished them from the comparison companies?*"[11] It boiled down to similarities in the characteristics of the CEOs of those companies.

Although *Good to Great* used different terms, all of the CEOs were what we would call "apostolic," or apostle-like.

They had egos and great ambition, but their ambition was mostly for their companies, not for themselves personally. They were humble and modest, yet fearless. They motivated people through inspired standards, not personal charisma or rank like their domineering CEO counterparts in other companies.

And they surrounded themselves with people who had talents and skills that complemented their own so that a leadership team was built that brought to the table at least some of the characteristics of the other "gifts" listed in Ephesians 4:11, that is, prophetic or perceptive, evangelistic or spreading good reports, teaching or communicating, and pastoral or compassionate. Often the team was in place even before the business plans were formulated, a practice Collins likened to "getting the right people on the bus."

We will look more closely at the definitions and purposes of these five-fold gifts in later chapters, but for now suffice it to say it looked to me like these winning CEOs were practicing a version of the Ephesians 4:11–16 model, albeit rough and incomplete.

A light went on.

What if, in fact, the five-fold gifts are for the marketplace and not just the church? This struck me as a very reasonable although revolutionary thought.

But where to start? Rarely was five-fold being applied with intentionality even in the church, much less in the marketplace.

---

11   Jim Collins, *Good to Great*, © 2002, HarperCollins Publishers, New York, NY, p.7, italics added.

Many companies profess to be run on biblical principles, but those usually center on Christian ethics and servant leadership, all of which are essential but in my view don't go far enough. It was surprising enough to me that there was no research I knew of that supports whether these principles work in the church. Could we find out through research of empirical evidence whether these principles work when applied outside the church?

I proposed this to Dr. Mulford, and he asked me to present the question to the School of Business faculty, which I did after a few weeks of preparation.

I was received cordially, and a healthy discussion ensued. The professors were interested in the concept, but clearly there was paradigm entrenchment to contend with. A stumbling block seemed to be a question of whether the idea of five-fold in the marketplace is hermeneutically[12] sound. I certainly appreciated the desire of those professors to be sure of truth and accuracy. The pursuit of truth is the key passion of the five-fold teacher, as we will see later, so they were being true to their calling.

It is true the Bible does not say specifically that the five-fold gifts are for anything other than the church. But neither does it specifically say they are *limited* to the church.[13] Rather that's just

---

12   "Hermeneutics" is the study of the interpretation of written texts. The term is inspired by the name of Hermes, the messenger of the gods in ancient Greek mythology. I've long thought that if Bible colleges had football teams, a good nickname for one of them would be "The Hermeneutics," a name bound to strike terror in the hearts of rival teams. Or maybe it would work for the debate team.

13   While this is true for Ephesians 4:11–16, 1 Corinthians 12:28 does say, "And in the church God has appointed first of all apostles, second prophets, third teachers, then workers of miracles, also those having gifts of healing, those able to help others, those with gifts of administration, and those speaking in different kinds of tongues." I do not take this as a statement of exclusivity for the church, and furthermore I will show beginning in the next chapter that God intended there to be no distinction between church and marketplace ministry anyway.

something we have assumed from the context and our traditional ways of thinking.

There are many things that are not specifically mentioned or listed in the Bible but are acceptable because they pass a test of being *compatible* with the Bible. As Dr. Mark Virkler says, "The Bible reveals God; it doesn't contain Him."

The idea that five-fold is for the church *and* the marketplace is compatible with the Bible. *My contention is that God did give the five-fold headship gifts to the church, and He did so in order for the church to use them in the world to help facilitate the spread of the Kingdom.* In subsequent chapters I will lay out my biblically based argument for this.

Ironically, while the Business School faculty were rightly debating hermeneutics, I had occasion during a stroll across the campus to engage in a brief conversation about this with Dr. Vinson Synan who at that time was Dean of the Regent University Divinity School. "Of course five-fold is for the marketplace," he said, almost as if it were a silly question. He thought it was a given.

In the end, the School of Business concluded that a properly conducted research project seemed impractical. It would have required a prodigious effort maintained over several years involving either the compilation of data from businesses that were using five-fold principles or convincing businesses to test it so that empirical evidence of effectiveness could be obtained under controlled conditions. Such companies would have been difficult if not impossible to find.

But the idea stayed with me.

WHAT'S HAPPENED SINCE THEN

During the intervening years I've learned that Dr. Vinson Synan isn't the only respected leader in the faith who agrees with the concept of five-fold ministry operating in the marketplace. A partial list includes those quoted or referenced here and there in this book, such as Dr. Mark Virkler, Dr. Lance Wallnau, Graham Cooke, Dr. C. Peter Wagner, Os Hillman, Dr. Bill Hamon, Randy Clark, Dr. Bruce Cook, Dr. John Mulford, Max Myers, and Rodney Odom, the senior leader at Grace Church in High Point, North Carolina, where my wife, Carol, and I now attend. There are others I know of from their writings, public statements, or conversations I have had with them. Those lists are just the tip of an iceberg because there are many others besides. In fact, I'd be surprised to find anyone of the caliber of these people now who would disagree.

Using business terms, Dr. Bill Hamon sees it this way (I especially like the first sentence.):

"Apostles are like the founders or entrepreneurs who launch divisions of God's enterprise on Earth. Prophets are like strategists who plan and evaluate how to meet Kingdom objectives. Evangelists are the sales managers who inspire their team to expand the business. Teachers may be likened to trainers who ground the workers in the principles, products and services of the organization. Pastors are similar to local business managers of units or branches who oversee the regular operations of their people, encourage them to meet their full potential, and help them work together as a team."[14]

Good to Great itself provides strong evidence in support of this. Furthermore, my own experience as a senior executive in multinational companies bears witness to the fact that when people are matched by their skill sets and talents (or call them giftings or gifts) to the requirements of a job, there is a whole lot more productivity and a lot less drama than otherwise.

---

14   Dr. Bill Hamon, *The Day of the Saints*, Destiny Image, Shippensburg, PA, 2002, pp. 269–270.

THE GRACE CHURCH "411 GROUP"

To top it all off, in October 2009 Rodney Odom started what he calls "The 411 Group" at Grace Church. Led by Rodney and his wife, Marcia, who ministers with him, it has since grown to about 60 people out of a church of about 350. Most have no official titles but simply bring their five-fold gifts to the table to support what God is doing in the church. They are *de facto* elders serving alongside the official board of elders established in the church's by-laws.

The unofficial charter of The 411 Group includes such statements as:

"The group is based on the listing of giftings in Ephesians 4:11. Everyone in the group has been invited because of their desire to see more of God and His Kingdom. The focus of the group will eventually be not just on Grace Church, but beyond. It is not a 'governing' group but is for those with a leadership calling on their lives. Our vision is to see what God is doing here at Grace and in the earth, and to join Him in that work."

At Grace Church, and in the marketplace, "We want leaders who understand the culture of Heaven. Who pray what Jesus is praying. Leaders who are a target for the presence of God, to bring the relentless Good News of the Kingdom."[15]

Profound transformation is taking place at Grace. God's presence and blessing is felt more than ever. There is a family atmosphere among the congregation, a sense of unity, and a growing spirit of love and joy.

Forming The 411 Group is one way the Lord has shown Rodney to employ the model of Ephesians 4:11–16. In using the group, he has not forsaken the counsel of the specifically appointed church elders in the governance of the institution. Indeed, he

---

15   Graham Cooke, speaking at the Think Brilliant Conference, Grace Church, High Point, NC, September 3, 2011.

recently expanded that board so that it, too, now has a broader representation of the five-fold gifts.

Rodney and Marcia also seek prophetic input and counsel from certain trusted and mature people outside our church, to some of whom they have made themselves spiritually accountable.

Most of the ministries of the church are not programs thought up and imposed by Rodney and the elders, but rather they sprang from the Holy Spirit led vision of various people in the congregation who felt called to propose them and/or lead them.

The church is growing in numbers, but that is almost beside the point. The real growth is in the spiritual maturity, competence, confidence and joy of the people, who have an increasingly better understanding of their calling and destiny. They are becoming better equipped. Their impact is being increasingly felt in the surrounding community and around the world where thousands of lives are being touched by what is happening here.

I know this is not a marketplace example. However, I do think ideally five-fold leadership starts in the church, and the church, through its "ministers" (us) who have practiced it there and have therefore become equipped to use it, should then apply it in the marketplace. Grace Church is an example of a church that understands this. I don't know what's next for the 411 Group, whether it will continue, morph into something else or cease to exist after a season. But it's what's needed at Grace Church for now.

An Epiphany and a Call to Arms: "The Five-fold Effect"

With all the agreement about it by leaders of the faith plus the evidence of the effectiveness of five-fold from *Good to Great* and other books, and with my own experience in business and now at our church, I finally realized: My vision was too small! To paraphrase a famous quote from the movie *Blazing Saddles*, "We don't need no stinking research!" We already know the answer. The application of five-fold ministry principles to the marketplace, with discipline and intentionality, led and powered by the Holy Spirit, is a valid concept.

What we do need is to publish this truth so it can be learned and practiced. As disciples of Jesus, being obedient to the Great Commission, we must now exercise apostolic authority as we engage and take dominion over the earth for the Kingdom, as God had intended Adam and Eve to do, moving outside the walls of our churches and into the marketplace.[16]

As the Nike advertisement says, let's "Just Do It!"

But before we just do it, let's take some time to understand what it is we're going to just do, why we're going to do it, and the implications it has for the church, our lives and the world.

I want to start by giving in the next few chapters what I believe is the biblical basis for the assertions made in this book. That, combined with such empirical evidence as we have that they are true (*Good to Great* and other anecdotal business examples, the experience of Grace Church, and my own observations from the marketplace), and the fact that it just makes sense and is Bible-compatible, should set the stage for a more in-depth explanation of the Ephesians 4 model and some detailed guidelines for how to apply it in your life.

---

16   I am struck by this statement of purpose by Dr. C. Peter Wagner: "Our theological bedrock is what has been known as Dominion Theology. This means that our divine mandate is to do whatever is necessary, by the power of the Holy Spirit, to retake the dominion of God's creation which Adam forfeited to Satan in the Garden of Eden. It is nothing less than seeing God's kingdom coming and His will being done here on earth as it is in heaven." (Excerpt from letter by Dr. C. Peter Wagner to his Global Harvest Ministries, May 31, 2007)

ACTIVATION EXERCISES

1. Does the argument presented here for the five-fold ministry gifts being for the church *and* the marketplace make sense to you? Do you agree with it?

2. If so, can you begin to think of how it might apply to any organizations you are involved in, whether at church or at work, or anywhere? List one or two such organizations and jot down your initial thoughts on how the five-fold model might be applied and/or might benefit the organization.

3. If you are not convinced, what are your biggest questions or reservations about this? Make a list and come back to it later after you've read more (I hope you're not so put off by the idea that you won't read on!).

CHAPTER 2

A Picture of the Church in the Marketplace

Deuteronomy 16:13–17, Ephesians 4:11–16, and Zechariah 2 — A Prophetic Sandwich

In a combination of the three scriptures above, from both the Old and New Testaments, God shows us what the ideal picture of the church in the marketplace looks like. There are other supporting scriptures as well, but these three seem to do a pretty good job. Because "Man does not live on bread alone but on every word that comes from the mouth of the Lord" (Deuteronomy 8:3b), I liken these three passages to a sort of prophetic sandwich. It is made up of two slices of "bread" (Ezekiel 4:9 bread, of course) with the "meat" in between (Figure 2–1).

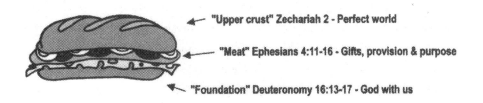

"Upper crust" Zechariah 2 - Perfect world

"Meat" Ephesians 4:11-16 - Gifts, provision & purpose

"Foundation" Deuteronomy 16:13-17 - God with us

Figure 2–1: "Prophetic Sandwich" Governance Model

The bread on the bottom, or the foundational slice, is Deuteronomy 16:13–17. It describes the inseparability of the church from the seven mountains of society as first ordained by God when laying out the rules Moses recorded for celebrating the Jewish festivals.

The meat in the middle is Ephesians 4:11–16, which is God's organizational strategy for how this is to function and which is also the meat of this book.[17]

The bread on top, which we could call the "upper crust," is Zechariah 2. Here the prophet describes what the "city," or the world, is supposed to look like when all this is working properly according to God's plan. No doubt there are still more scriptures that could provide "lettuce and tomato" to garnish the sandwich, as well as a suitable condiment. Probably mustard since this is a biblical sandwich after all. That is, unless we rely on the well-known apocryphal aphorism, "Man cannot live on bread alone; he must have peanut butter,"[18] in which case we might also want some grape jelly.[19]

In this chapter we will discuss the passage from Deuteronomy. In the next chapter we will look at Zechariah 2. Then the rest of

---

17   Those who have the meat shall inherit the earth.

18   This saying, often ascribed to President Grover A. Cleveland even though peanut butter did not yet exist during his Administration, has spread, so to speak, throughout the culture, reportedly being used by such notables as Brother Dave Gardner and Bill Cosby, as well as a supermarket in St. Louis and in the background of a Jefferson Airplane recording.

19   Those who have the peanut butter and jelly shall inherit the earth?

the book will be devoted to the meat, the Ephesians 4 model and how to apply it.

A Meditation on Deuteronomy 16:13–17

Read this passage carefully. Moses is expressing the words of God as he lays out the rules for observing the Jewish festivals.

13 Celebrate the Feast of Tabernacles for seven days after you have gathered the produce of your threshing floor and your winepress. 14 Be joyful at your Feast—you, your sons and daughters, your menservants and maidservants, and the Levites, the aliens, the fatherless and the widows who live in your towns. 15 For seven days celebrate the Feast to the Lord your God at the place the Lord will choose. For the Lord your God will bless you in all your harvest and in all the work of your hands, and your joy will be complete.

16 Three times a year all your men must appear before the Lord your God at the place he will choose: at the Feast of Unleavened Bread, the Feast of Weeks and the Feast of Tabernacles. No man should appear before the Lord empty-handed: 17 Each of you must bring a gift in proportion to the way the Lord your God has blessed you.

First, notice the emphasis on the Feast of Tabernacles. Three feasts are discussed here and in preceding verses, but the Feast of Tabernacles is singled out for the most attention. I suspect that's because it's the one that prophesies what God has been most longing for and looking forward to.[20]

---

20   Also see Leviticus 23:33–44.

Spirit, Word and Life — A Seamless Tapestry

Let's delve into this Scripture.

"After you have gathered the produce of your threshing floor and your winepress." (v. 13): What is He talking about? "The produce" of course represents business and commerce.

"The aliens . . . who live in your towns" (v.14): The law required that foreigners be welcomed and protected. In modern terms, these feasts, observances, and works of the Lord are for everybody, not just church members, whether they are Israelite or Christian. God was speaking to the church—Israel at that time, us today—and saying there is not, nor should there be, any separation between the church (religious or spiritual life) and the marketplace (where all life is lived).[21] The "marketplace" is all areas of a society's life, not just business and commerce.

"For seven days *celebrate*" (v.15): This is the time set aside to commemorate, but the rest of the year this plan is to be lived out as everyday life, continually giving thanks for the bounty God has provided.

"At the place *the Lord will choose*" (v.15–16): It's all about Him and His glory, not our plans or our economy, etc. He is the ruler. He sets the agenda.

There is a promise given with these commands: Honor and obey Him, and He "will bless you in all your harvest and in all the work of your hands, and your joy will be complete" (v.15).

"The work of your hands" (v.15) means all that you do in the marketplace as well as in your personal life. "Work" is not limited to what you do at the factory or at the office, but includes everything from hobbies to charity and church work, civic volunteer work, washing the dishes, doing the laundry, mowing the lawn, and building a tree house for your kids.

---

21 Do not misunderstand. The Bible does not prescribe, nor do I advocate, a state religion. The Bible does describe, however, a government that operates on biblical principles and that protects freedom of worship for everyone.

Notice the wording here. He doesn't say "*your* work," but "the work of your hands." That means work as prepared by God beforehand. "For we are God's workmanship[22], created in Christ Jesus to do good works, which God prepared in advance for us to do" (Ephesians 2:10). Again, it is His agenda.

"All your men must appear before the Lord" (v.16): Men have first responsibility for provision, protection and identity of the people. I know that is not limited to men, and many women were engaged in commerce in Old Testament Israel. We have only to recall the Virtuous Woman in Proverbs 31:10–31 to understand that. But "men" was the custom of expression in Old Testament Israel. And notice, it says *all* your men. Nobody had an excuse to stay home during these festivals!

It didn't mean just the rank and file members of society, excusing those too important to be bothered. It definitely included the leaders, the movers and shakers. *These are the people occupying the higher levels of the seven mountains of influence, providing direction and results throughout* all *areas of society, guided by God's precepts. It is not just limited to business.* For me, this is the key idea of this Scripture as it relates to how God sees His plan in action on the earth and how we are to respond with a view toward doing what we see God doing in weaving the seamless tapestry.

DEDICATING AND USING OUR GIFTS

"No man should appear before the Lord empty-handed."(V.16): We need to understand that no man is empty-handed in the first place. The Lord has blessed each of us with gifts

---

22   Or "masterpiece" in the New Living Translation (NLT). Retired pastor, Walter Isbill, writes on his Website: "There is a fabulously interesting Greek word, '*poema*,' which the King James translators render as 'workmanship.' From this word we get our English word, 'poem.' Literally, it means to me that we Christians are God's poems written by the very hand of God. To meditate upon this simply makes my day!" (http://wbisbill.hubpages.com/hub/I-Am-Gods-Poem)

already and asks that these gifts be used in His service, everywhere. This understanding helps us to interpret the command, **"Each of you must *bring a gift in proportion to the way the Lord your God has blessed you*"** (v.17, or, "Every man shall give as he is able, according to the blessing of the Lord thy God which he hath given thee" [KJV]).

Here God is not talking mostly about animals to be sacrificed, or even about tithing, although all that is part of it, i.e., giving out of your increase. Rather, and here's a revelation, He is talking about talent and skill being used for the benefit of the whole body of the society. Recall 1 Peter 4:10. "Each one should use whatever gift he has received to serve others, faithfully administering God's grace in its various forms." Think also of the five-fold gifts (Ephesians 4:11–16), plus service and administration (1 Corinthians 12:28), the nine gifts of the Holy Spirit (1 Corinthians 12:7–11), and the seven motivational gifts (Rom. 12:3–8). We should be using them as if we were serving the Lord with them and be ready on the feast occasions, or actually any time and place He asks, to give an account.

WESTERN VERSUS HEBREW MIND-SET

In Deuteronomy 16:13–17 we see a picture of a society where the church and Godly principles are employed at all levels, fully integrated into the seven mountains. This is very different from our Western mind-set, which is still highly influenced by ancient Greek philosophy. The Greeks, typified by Plato, believed that everything is centered on man. Hence the philosophies of humanism and rationalism. However, for the Israelites, as it should be for us, God is at the center.

Plato taught that there is a separation between the spiritual realm and the natural realm and that, therefore, work, or the marketplace, is separate from (and inferior to) the spiritual. Deuteronomy 16 and many other Scriptures paint a very different picture. As Dr. C. Peter Wagner puts it, the

"Hebrews see both the spiritual and the natural (including work) realms as one entity under the hand of God. The conclusion that can be derived from the Hebrew perspective is that our work is a form of ministry. It is as sacred as singing in the choir. I know that this can be hard to agree with at first, because we have been programmed with the Greek mind-set. But the more we can switch our paradigm to the Hebrew mind-set, the better we will understand the church in the workplace."[23]

Figure 2–2 is a simple representation of this concept.

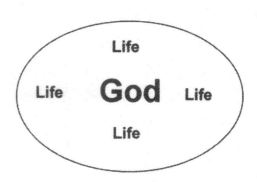

Figure 2–2: The Hebrew Mind-set

In summary, Deuteronomy 16 shows us that there is not, nor should there be, any separation between the church and the marketplace. Again, the "marketplace" is all areas of a society's life, not just business and commerce.

In Chapter 3 we will look at the "upper crust" of our prophetic sandwich as we read the second chapter of Zechariah and see a remarkable picture of what a truly Godly world is supposed to look like when this truth is practiced. After that, we will look more closely at the Ephesians 4 model.

---

23   C. Peter Wagner, *The Church in the Workplace,* Regal Books, Ventura CA, 2006, p. 15.

ACTIVATION EXERCISES

1. Meditate on Deuteronomy 16:13–17. Does the analysis and interpretation offered here make sense and seem real to you?

2. Do you feel you have a Greek mind-set or a Hebrew mind-set when it comes to thinking about the church in the workplace? If more Greek and you wish to change, confess this to God, repent (change the way you think about it), pray and ask God to help you see it His way. (And you are not allowed to say, "It's all Greek to me.")

3. Ask one or two trusted friends (including your spouse) to read this chapter and discuss it with you. Compare their "take" on it with yours. What other observations come from the discussion? (This is not a cleverly disguised trick to get you to buy two more books. You can lend them your copy. But I wouldn't mind if they got their own copies. What a great gift, and Christmas and birthdays are always right around the corner!)

CHAPTER 3

The Ultimate Godly City

The (minor) Prophet Zechariah Explains It All to You

Well, maybe he doesn't explain all of it, but certainly a lot, which is not bad for a minor prophet.

Ralph and Marie

"Where are you off to?" asked Ralph, watching his wife, Marie, in bathing suit and flip flops cramming stuff into her beach bag in their rented vacation cottage at the beach.

"I thought I might go to, oh, you know, the beach," she said. "You should come too."

"I'll be along after I check my e-mail. Do you have a book to read?"

He knew she did, but he wanted to deflect her annoyance that he couldn't keep from working a little even while they were on vacation. Her book had a black cover, but he couldn't read the title from where he stood sipping coffee in the little kitchenette.

"Yes," she said, "today I'll be reading the minor prophets."

"I don't think that one's made the New York Times Bestseller list yet, but have fun. I'll come out there soon."

Marie adjusted her new straw hat and flip flopped out. Ralph opened his laptop, went to Amazon.com and searched for *The Miner Prophets*. He figured it was probably a book about some folks in West Virginia who predicted coal mine disasters. It wasn't listed.

Of course, the book Marie carried was a Bible. If she sat on the beach reading the book of Zechariah she was treated to more drama than the average beach reading novel offers as well as a beautiful picture of what a Godly city looks like. Here is the "upper crust" of our prophetic sandwich.

WHAT GOD SHOWED ZECHARIAH (AND MARIE)

1 Then I looked up—and there before me was a man with a measuring line in his hand! 2 I asked, "Where are you going?" He answered me, "To measure Jerusalem, to find out how wide and how long it is."

3 Then the angel who was speaking to me left, and another angel came to meet him 4 and said to him: "Run, tell that young man, **`Jerusalem will be a city without walls because of the great number of men and livestock in it. 5 And I myself will be a wall of fire around it,' declares the Lord, `and I will be its glory within.'**

6 "Come! Come! Flee from the land of the north," declares the Lord, "for I have scattered you to the four winds of heaven," declares the Lord.

7 "Come, O Zion! **Escape, you who live in the Daughter of Babylon!"** 8 For this is what the Lord Almighty says: "After he has honored me and has sent me against the nations that have plundered you—for whoever touches you touches the apple of his eye— 9 I will surely raise my hand against them so that their slaves will plunder them. Then you will know that the Lord Almighty has sent me.

10 "Shout and be glad, O Daughter of Zion. **For I am coming, and *I will live among you*,"** declares the Lord. **11 "Many nations will be joined with the Lord in that day and will become my people.** *I will live among you* **and you will know that the Lord Almighty has sent me to you.** 12 The Lord will inherit Judah as his portion in the holy land and will again choose Jerusalem. 13 Be still before the Lord, all mankind, because he has roused himself from his holy dwelling" (Zechariah 2, written around 518 BC, bold and italics added).

At first reading, this seems merely another prophecy about God calling the Jewish people home from exile, having forgiven them for their disobedience one more time, and promising to live among them again. It is all that, but also it is so much more!

It starts on a positive and exciting note. Zechariah sees some guy getting ready to measure Jerusalem! Oh, but it turns out he is a young man and therefore presumably a little naive, but he is obviously overcome by the brilliant spectacle of the city he finds himself in. Besides, isn't there something traditional about measuring cities? Or at least temples, which were central to the life of the city (See Revelation 11:1–2, 1 Kings 6, *et al*). Usually, it was about measuring for the building of a wall around the city, important because walls were a city's protection. So we can chuckle at this young man, but we can still admire his zeal.

But it's just a set up for what God really wants to say: "Thanks for your enthusiasm, but save yourself the trouble. It's too big. In fact it's endless. Try measuring that! Now let me tell you about it."

For our purposes here, I think what God wants to say about it is in the parts in bold below.

"Jerusalem will be a city without walls because of the great number of men and livestock in it." (v.4b): "Men" refers to society. "Livestock" refers to business or commerce. The seven mountains of influence are encompassed in that. "Great number" means the city is for the whole world, and therefore there is no need for conventional walls. God's provisions are endless and can't be contained.

"Come, O Zion! Escape, you who live in the Daughter of Babylon!" (v.7): This is a call for believers to come out of the world (not literally, but by putting Godly things ahead of worldly things) and join the Kingdom of God. As more and more do so, the city gets bigger and bigger in order to accommodate everyone. There is room enough for all. As my wife, Carol, observes, "There was no room in the inn for Jesus, but He has made provision for all who would come now."

"And I myself will be a wall of fire around it, declares the Lord, and I will be its glory within." (v.5): It is a city without boundaries, protected by a flame of God. The flame is not to keep the inhabitants in, nor is it to keep out those whose rightful place is in the city, including foreigners. It is to keep out evil and evil people and to dispense justice and mercy.[24]

"Many nations will be joined with the Lord in that day and will become my people." (v.11a): The Lord is calling *all* people, Jews and Gentiles alike, to be saved and to live in His city (See Romans 8:28–30). If everyone "will become my people," it

---

24   "Therefore, since we are receiving a kingdom that cannot be shaken, let us be thankful, and so worship God acceptably with reverence and awe, for our 'God is a consuming fire.'" (Hebrews 12:28–29)

means either that there will be no more nations or that there will be one huge nation, even if within it there may still be political boundary lines for Man's convenience. And God is in the midst of the marketplace ("men and livestock"), and "many nations" (and their commerce) are joined there with the Lord, forming the one big nation.[25]

"**'For I am coming, and *I will live among you,*'** declares the Lord." (v.10) and "*I will live among you* **and you will know that the Lord Almighty has sent me to you.**" (v.11b): Here again is Jesus' promise that He will live among us forever.

So what we have here is a picture, and a promise, of what life is to be like when God's plan is fulfilled. Zechariah 2 is what the "city" looks like when it's working properly according to God's plan. The whole world is included. God is in our midst, the Holy Spirit guiding our steps but not usurping our free will. We go about our lives in peace and harmony, protected from evil. This is when "every knee bows and every tongue confesses that Jesus Christ is Lord" (Philippians 2:10–11[26]). God and we enjoy His heart's desire, an intimate relationship with us, His creation. God gets all the glory.

I don't think that's a picture of Heaven, because the Bible doesn't say we all have to die before Zechariah's vision comes to pass. I think it's a picture of the Eden God always intended for Adam and Eve, and therefore us, when He charged them with taking dominion over the earth! So maybe we or our descendants will see this before "the end of the age."

A favorite Scripture of mine that corroborates this is the well-

---

25 This concept may be uncomfortable for people who, like me, are skeptical about the concept of "world government" and its implied surrender of national sovereignty to an international authority. However, the sovereignty surrendered to in the nation described here is God's only, and I'm more than willing to live in that place.

26 Also see Isaiah 45:23 and Romans 14:11.

known Isaiah 60, written around 700 BC, about 200 years before Zechariah. It's the one that starts, "Arise, shine, for your light has come, and the glory of the Lord rises upon you." It goes on to talk about nations coming to your light, the wealth of nations coming to you, and so on. Stop here for a moment and read Isaiah 60 now. You will feel really good afterwards. I'll bet you know of some other passages like this too.

I believe this is also what Paul was describing in Ephesians 2:19–22 (italics added):

"Consequently, you are no longer foreigners and aliens, but fellow citizens with God's people and members of God's household, built on the foundation of the *apostles and prophets*, with Christ Jesus himself as the chief cornerstone. In him the whole building is joined together and rises to become a holy temple in the Lord. And in him you too are being built together to become a dwelling in which God lives by his Spirit."

This language is strikingly similar to Ephesians 4:11–16, which we will explore further beginning in Chapter 4. Paul is talking here about the church, yes, but a church inseparable from society, and therefore a nation, in which God lives by His Spirit, as we first saw in Deuteronomy 16. In the late 1970s at a Lydia conference in Ridgecrest, North Carolina, the Lord gave this word to Carol: "As Jesus is the foundation of the church, the church is the foundation of the nation."

Here I am not talking about the church as an organized, monolithic institution, *per se*. As I said in the Introduction, such a thing doesn't exist. I'm talking about the church as billions of believers, based in millions of local churches but living and operating in the world, taught and led by apostles, prophets, pastors, teachers and evangelists who have equipped these believers to use those same five-fold gifts to change the atmosphere in their own individual areas of influence at work, play and everyday life.

A scripture that neatly ties together for us the pictures in Deuteronomy 16 and Zechariah 2 is Nahum 1:15. Nahum was another minor prophet, writing in about 615 BC. While warning Nineveh, which had fallen back into sin 150 years after heeding Jonah's warning, Nahum had a word of reassurance for Judah that encapsulates God's commands and promises for how we are supposed to live:

"Behold upon the mountains the feet of him that bringeth good tidings, that publisheth peace! O Judah, *keep thy solemn feasts, perform thy vows: for the wicked shall no more pass through thee; he is utterly cut off*" (KJV, italics added).

I like the King James Version here because of the imagery of evil being "utterly cut off."

If we who are the church take dominion over the seven mountains, we'll be well on our way toward realizing the picture in Zechariah 2.[27]

Back to Ralph

Ralph missed all this. But he knew what he was going to say to Marie when he finally joined her on the beach about an hour later. "Honey, I think I misunderstood when you told me what book you were reading. I misspelled the key word. I bet they're going to make it into a new reality show on TV. It's 'The Minor Prophets,' and it's about a bunch of high school kids in Beverly Hills who can predict the future."

Without bothering to look up, Marie kicked sand at him.

---

27   Again, I'm not talking about the church as an institution taking over the world. That's been tried, and it's a bad idea. And besides, the "religion mountain" is not a "Christian mountain." It is *all* religion or faith-based influence, not just Christian. So don't get a picture in your mind of a Christian religion mountain rising up and devouring the other 6 mountains, like Aaron's rod turning into a snake and eating Pharaoh's rods(Exodus 7:10–12). No, it's about what we do individually and together as the body of Christ, not The Amalgamated Jesus Corporation.

ACTIVATION EXERCISES

1. Read Zechariah 2 again, using more than one translation, and meditate on it. Ask the Holy Spirit to show you what He would like you to see in it. How would you like to live life among the "upper crust"?

2. Read Isaiah 60 the same way. What thoughts, hopes, and dreams does it spark in you?

3. As with the previous chapter, ask one or two trusted friends to read this chapter and discuss it with you. What do they think? Do they have their own copies of the book yet? What are they waiting for?

CHAPTER 4

THE EPHESIANS 4 MODEL OF TRANSFORMATIONAL LEADERSHIP

Here's the meat in the middle. As we've seen, Ephesians 4:11–16 is the passage where Paul lays out God's plan and provision for how the church, and by extension, any organization or endeavor involving more than one person, is to operate. It is called the five-fold ministry model, and it is the meat (or the peanut butter) of our prophetic sandwich. It is the central ingredient that can propel us toward our own destiny and toward seven mountain dominion and bring us closer to realizing Zechariah's vision.

Or, less cosmically, but more importantly as an immediate practical matter, it can make our organizations supernaturally productive.

11 And He Himself gave some to be apostles, some prophets, some evangelists, and some pastors and teachers, [12] for the equipping of the saints for the work of ministry, for the edifying of the body of Christ, [13] till we all come to the unity of the faith and of the knowledge of the Son of God, to a perfect man, to the measure of the stature of the fullness of Christ;

[14] that we should no longer be children, tossed to and fro and carried about with every wind of doctrine, by the trickery of men, in the cunning craftiness of deceitful plotting, [15] but, speaking the truth in love, may grow up in all things into Him who is the head—Christ— [16] from whom the whole body, joined and knit together by what every joint supplies, according to the effective working by which every part does its share, causes growth of the body for the edifying of itself in love (NKJV).

Here's an outline of the plan:

- Provision: God provided leadership via the five-fold ministry (v. 11, human servant leaders—Apostles, prophets, pastors, teachers and evangelists—empowered and led by the Holy Spirit), to administer the Purpose.
- Purpose: The equipping of the saints to do the work of the ministry (v. 12a), so that...
- Result: The vision of His church is realized (vv. 12b–16).

Wow! You mean that's it? The whole plan for how the church should be led, and why, right there in six verses and hardly anywhere else in the Bible? There are other places these gifts are mentioned (Romans 12:28 and Ephesians 2:19–22, for example),[28], [29] so I think that confirms the importance of it, but, yes, here is the only place it's all together in one package like this.

---

28   Romans 12:28 comes close when it says, "And in the church God has appointed first of all apostles, second prophets, third teachers, then workers of miracles, also those having gifts of healing, those able to help others, those with gifts of administration, and those speaking in different kinds of tongues," and elsewhere we find that the church rests on the apostles and prophets, with Jesus as the cornerstone

29   "Consequently, you are no longer foreigners and aliens, but fellow citizens with God's people and members of God's household, 20 *built on the foundation of the apostles and prophets, with Christ Jesus himself as the chief cornerstone.* 21In him the whole building is joined together and rises to become a holy temple in the Lord. 22 And in him you too are being built together to become a dwelling in which God lives by his Spirit." Eph. 2:19–22 (NIV, italics added)

In Figure 4–1, look again at the simplified model in the diagram we first saw in the Introduction.

Figure 4–1: Five-Fold Leadership Model for Church

Here we have the five gifts arrayed in a circle that represents eternal wholeness or completeness, as well as mutual love, much like the symbolism of a wedding band. The gifts are listed clockwise in the order they are mentioned in Ephesians 4:11 (There is no particular rationale for clockwise or counterclockwise.), forming a protective circle around the church body they lead. The connecting lines should be thought of as "access lines," and they speak of the five gifts working together interdependently, supporting each other and investing into the lives of the members of the church body or congregation (the "saints"). Via the access lines, people can exercise the multiple giftings they have and can move freely from current roles to others as they grow and move toward their destiny and calling and as seasons change in the vision, growth, and development of the body.

Because apostolic leaders do not lord it over their people, a circular arrangement is more illustrative than a traditional organization chart with a hierarchy of boxes for various positions. All the leaders and members are of equal importance, and there is no superiority or inferiority involved, the only "hierarchy" being about greater or less authority, responsibility, maturity and growth.[30] (However, organization charts do have practical value, as we'll see later.)

Nothing about the diagram should be construed as a barrier to people coming to the church or as a barrier keeping its members from going out into the world to impact the marketplace, having been well-equipped by the leadership.

Please note I am not saying a church or any other organization should be rigidly led by a five person committee each of whom has one of these five gifts, only that ideally all five gifts should be represented in the leadership. I offer the diagram only as a convenient aid to thinking about apostolic or five-fold ministry or leadership. You can think of it as an icon like the one I've included on the first page of each chapter of the book. [31]

IT'S FOR ALL ORGANIZATIONS

We've seen that this is God's model and plan for church governance and that it is for today. It applies in the marketplace

---

30   See 1 Corinthians 12:14–31, especially v. 14: "Now the body is not made up of one part but of many." and vv. 21–22: "The eye cannot say to the hand, 'I don't need you!' And the head cannot say to the feet, I don't need you!' On the contrary, those parts of the body that seem to be weaker are indispensable."

31   This diagram reminds me of the infamous Benzene Ring we all heard about in high school chemistry. Not being as interested in chemistry as I should have been, I always felt the Benzene Ring might just as well describe the organized theft of German luxury automobiles. For today, however, the Benzene Ring is a good example from nature of the utter interdependence of constituent elements acting together for mutual benefit in maintaining the healthy integrity of the compound, much like a healthy apostolic organization. (Image from 2B1st Consulting. Used with permission.)

Benzene Ring (C_6H_6)

as well. How do we know this? Let's break it down using its own language.

The key line is "for the equipping of the saints for the work of ministry" (or "service" in about half of the translations). We, the believers, are the "saints." It simply means we are sanctified (set apart for sacred use) by God because of our belief in Jesus.[32] Many Christians still think of themselves as sinners. This is wrong because we are "new creatures" no longer under the control of sin.[33] Yes, we do make mistakes and sin from time to time, and there may be old sin habits and thought patterns that are still being broken, with God's help, but that no longer describes who we are. Without arrogance or boasting (except about Jesus), we should walk in the victory Jesus purchased for us.

We are saints not only on Sunday but also every day of the week as we go about our lives and our work. Each of us is performing his or her "saintly" activity, or making a saintly contribution, somewhere at some level on one or more of the seven mountains of influence. That activity, in addition to being a witness for Christ, consists of works of service to others, which is our ministry. Does this include charitable work, or "church work"? Yes, but much more often it is any service we perform for another person, whether it is a boss, an employee, a relative, a friend, or a stranger. "As you go" means that it is to be a lifestyle, not just a set of good deeds.[34]

---

32   In the NIV translation of the Bible, there are 68 references to "saints," each one referring to ordinary believers. Two good examples are Psalms 85:8, "I will listen to what God the Lord will say; he promises peace to his people, his saints—but let them not return to folly," and Romans 1:7, "To all in Rome who are loved by God and called to be saints: Grace and peace to you from God our Father and from the Lord Jesus Christ."

33   "Therefore, if anyone is in Christ, he is a new creation; the old has gone, the new has come!" (2 Corinthians 5:17)

34   See Matthew 10:7, "As you go, preach this message: 'The kingdom of heaven is near.'" Jesus' meaning here is the same.

If you wonder what your "ministry" is, that is it. It's not a mysterious calling you need to wait for God to show you. It's right in front of you. It's doing the thing at hand. That is not to say you don't already have a calling into one or more focal areas of service or ministry, but rather that you are doing ministry, being a minister or servant, whenever you work with someone.

Dr. Bill Hamon puts it this way:

"In the early New Testament Church the word *minister* was not used as the title of a clergy position but of Saints who ministered the life of Christ and power of God in the Church and to the world. Ministers in the marketplace are the Saints whose livelihood is outside the walls of the local church. Every true Saint has the right and authority to manifest the life of Christ and to minister the supernatural power of God."[35]

We've already seen that in God's eyes there is no separation between "church" (we, the body) and society (the marketplace). Thus, "edifying (the building up) of the body of Christ" is the building up of our whole godly society. That is transformational. It includes your local church, as well as any other specific organization or endeavor, but it is not limited to that.

WHY DID GOD GIVE THE FIVE-FOLD GIFTS?

We know God is a God of love. He is in fact love itself (or Himself), love so strong as to have created the universe with only a word. Love needs an object. The universe and Man, God's creations, are the objects of His love. But what objects were there before time began? William P. (Paul) Young, author of the phenomenally best selling book, *The Shack*, describes a way he likes to think of the Trinity, or the relationship between Father God, Jesus the Son, and the Holy Spirit. He sees them before the

---

35   Dr. Bill Hamon, *The Day of the Saints*, Destiny Image, Shippensburg, PA, 2002, p. 409.

beginning of time doing a sort of circle dance with one another and exhibiting "other-centered love." Each was, and is, the object of the others' love.[36] I find this concept of other-centered love to be a perfect added dimension to the way I think about who God is and about the perfect relationship between the three parts of the Godhead.

By creating the universe and Man, God has invited us into His eternal dance circle. Being created in His image, we too are designed to practice other-centered love. In fact, when asked what is the greatest commandment, "Jesus replied: 'Love the Lord your God with all your heart and with all your soul and with all your mind.' This is the first and greatest commandment. And the second is like it: 'Love your neighbor as yourself.' All the Law and the Prophets hang on these two commandments" (Matthew 22:37–40).

I submit that the five-fold gifts were given in order to facilitate our practice of these commandments as we interact with each other for the building up of the church or for any other righteous organizational purpose. Each one of the five needs and also supports the others. They are to prefer one another and to defer to one another, just as lovers do. Service, ministry, and servant leadership all embody the idea of other-centered love.

Each member of the Trinity contributes something unique and essential to the whole. The Father offers vision, security and protection, identity and value, and provision for His people. The Son offers Divine friendship, companionship, open communication, and intercession for us with the Father. The Holy Spirit offers comfort, guidance and teaching. In so doing, together they perfectly meet the specific needs of our bodies, our souls, and our spirits, respectively.

In the same way, as we will see more clearly later, each of the

---

36   William P. (Paul) Young speaking at Grace Church, High Point, NC, January 9, 2011

five-fold gifts contains a unique and essential set of characteristics that together satisfy the needs of bodies of people who come together for mutual benefit. As with the Trinity, the relationship among the five must be one of other-centered love in order for them to be effective. This is represented in Figure 4–2.

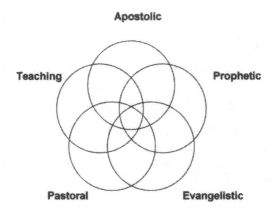

Figure 4–2: The Other-Centered Love "Dance" of Five-Fold Ministry

While remaining different from each other, each of the five is intimately engaged with the others, providing a unique blend of deference and leadership that depends on supernatural grace to work properly. Keeping to the dance analogy, clearly, no one is worried about his or her toes being stepped on! This goes way beyond the fact that the five-fold gifts, like the Trinity, fit together like a perfect puzzle and are responsible to see that the members of a body of people also fit and work together as perfectly as is possible for humans to do. It is love that drives it. Love provides the inspiration to bring it to life and for it to work as perfectly as it is designed.[37]

So Where Do I Fit In?

We may think Ephesians 4:11 is speaking only of the *offices*

---

37   This would be a good time to stop and read 1 Corinthians 13, "the love chapter," as a description of how we are supposed to treat each other in our relationships everywhere—at home, in church and in the marketplace.

of apostle, prophet, and so on. However, we also know that the apostolic and prophetic giftings and functions are in operation today, along with those of evangelist, pastor and teacher, among people we would not necessarily say are apostles or prophets, i.e., that they have that office. I submit that if you are put into an apostolic role, or a prophetic role, or any of the others, for a season or a task, then for that season, task and purpose, you are an apostle, a prophet, a teacher, a pastor or an evangelist. That is your role in the transforming of your organization from ordinary to extraordinary. In fact, you might be more than one simultaneously, according to the relationships, circumstances and needs within which you are functioning. We'll expand on this later.

NOT A NEW PLAN

I further submit that this model has actually been in effect from the Beginning. It has always been God's way of providing the resources for Man's successful life on earth. Let's go to the Old Testament for evidence.

OLD TESTAMENT ROOTS

Were there apostles, prophets, evangelists, pastors and teachers in the Old Testament? We know there were prophets galore! These were the people who "interpreted the divine will and purpose in inspired preaching and teaching."[38] And, yes, all of the other four were there as well, even though the word "apostle" itself does not appear in the Old Testament, nor does "evangelist." The word "pastor" is not in the NIV Old Testament but does appear eight times in the King James Version. "Teacher" appears in the Old Testament several times.

However, the argument does not rest on whether those titles

---

38   Paraphrasing the definition used in the Amplified Version of the Bible in 1 Corinthians 14:1 and many other places. "Amplified"® The Lockman Foundation.

were used. We can base it on the way the Bible describes the missions and assignments of the various chosen leaders. There are many examples of all five. Adam was an apostle when God created him to take dominion over the earth. Moses was an apostle, "the sent one," when God sent him to lead the rescue of His people from Egypt, and then he was also a prophet as he led them for the next 40 years. Aaron was a teacher when he explained to the people about manna and quail. Aaron and other priests were teachers of the law, as was Ezra later. Moses' father-in-law, Jethro, prophetically advised Moses on a strategy for delegating his leadership duties so as not to kill himself with overwork (Exodus 18:13–26). Aaron spoke prophetically to Pharaoh as Moses' mouthpiece, using words he received from God.

In Nehemiah 8, we see Nehemiah the apostle sent to rebuild the wall of Jerusalem; Ezra the priest and scribe finding the Book of the Law of Moses, leading worship and reading it to the people as a teacher; the Levites, 13 of whom are named, teaching the people from the Book, and then pastorally calming those who were grieving over having forsaken the Law for so long, after Nehemiah said, "Do not grieve, for the joy of the Lord is your strength" (v. 10b).

I'm not sure if there were evangelists, *per se*, because the Israelites were never a proselytizing people. However, they did welcome Gentiles who wanted to convert, and the Old Testament makes it clear they were to welcome and protect foreigners. Solomon asked God to answer the prayers of any foreigners who came to the temple.[39] It stands to reason there were Jews, maybe

---

39 "As for the foreigner who does not belong to your people Israel but has come from a distant land because of your great name and your mighty hand and your outstretched arm—when he comes and prays toward this temple, then hear from heaven, your dwelling place, and do whatever the foreigner asks of you, so that all the peoples of the earth may know your name and fear you, as do your own people Israel, and may know that this house I have built bears your Name." (2 Chronicles 6:32–33)

some of the priests, assigned to help such people both pastorally and evangelistically.

Earlier in the wilderness no doubt the priests performed other pastoral duties from time to time, helping the people to overcome confusion and disappointment during their time there, including helping to convince them not to return to Egypt every time a crisis occurred. Maybe that was evangelistic too—not that the Israelites wanted to become Egyptians, but as they learned how to be a free people after 400 years of slavery they needed encouragement by being reminded of the good news of the Promised Land that awaited.

GOD WAS INVOLVED IN EVERYTHING

Not only was God involved in Old Testament religious life, but also education, family, and government. Arts and entertainment centered on the passing down of God stories from generation to generation and worshipping Him with music and dancing. King David was a musician, poet and songwriter. He presided over 24 hour worship for 30 years by thousands of trained musicians using instruments he caused to be built. Both 2 Kings 24 and Jeremiah 24 record Nebuchadnezzar's deportation of 1,000 craftsmen and artisans from Jerusalem to Babylon, so clearly they were an important part of Jewish society. Media in the form of scrolls and stone tablets recorded these stories.

Was God involved in business and commerce? For the answer we have only to look again at such passages as Deuteronomy 16:13–17 and at Leviticus 23:33–44 where the leaders of all the "seven mountains" of the day were commanded to be present and make offerings during the appointed festivals, especially the Feast of Tabernacles, commemorating God's role in the harvest, which is commerce (See Chapter 2). We can infer something of how highly God regarded commerce when we also review Proverbs 31:10–31, the aspirational description of the virtuous, blessed and highly favored woman very much involved in business:

She considers a field and buys it; out of her earnings she plants a vineyard (v. 16).

She sees that her trading is profitable, and her lamp does not go out at night (v. 18).

She makes linen garments and sells them, and supplies the merchants with sashes (v. 24).

So we can see that Ephesians 4:11–16 is not a new plan. From the very Beginning, God appointed apostles, prophets, evangelists, pastors and teachers to lead and to facilitate the healthy and Godly functioning of Jewish society.

Transition to New Testament Times

All of those ministries carried over into the New Testament times in which we live today. Let's see what that looks like.

Visitation versus Habitation

In both the Old and New Testaments God usually carried out His plans through people, just as He does today. However, in the Old Testament the Holy Spirit didn't dwell in each person. Instead, He usually only touched certain ones to empower them for certain tasks, and on those occasions when Holy Spirit did fall on all the people, it was only temporary to fulfill a specific purpose. An important difference today is that instead of God working through people touched for certain purposes, either temporarily or for a lifetime, believers are *all* now permanently touched because the Holy Spirit dwells in each of us.

A New Kind of Apostle

Another difference is the added dimension Jesus created for the position of apostle. "Apostle" was a military term used by both the Greeks and the Romans to refer to an ambassador sent from the government of a conquering country to the conquered country.

It was the apostle's job to change the culture of the conquered country so that it resembled his own so that when the conquering ruler visited he would feel at home. Otherwise, according to the prevailing thought, what was the point of expanding one's empire?

Military apostles did that by imposing governmental organization and laws like those at home, introducing their own language and cultural practices, and even changing the road systems.

To the disappointment of many Jews who were expecting a Messiah who would act like a military ruler and overthrow the Romans, Jesus chose to *offer* the Kingdom rather than to *impose* it. Yet His aims were the same. In establishing His own apostles along with the other four of the five-fold ministries, Jesus created a self-replicating ambassadorship whose mission was, and is, to represent the Kingdom on Earth and to establish its culture here so that Jesus will recognize it as His when He returns for us, His church. To Him, it will look a lot like Heaven.[40]

JESUS THE MARKETPLACE MINISTER

Because the Bible records nothing of Joseph's life after the episode in the temple when Jesus was 12 (Luke 2:41–52), we usually assume he died sometime before Jesus' ministry began. It therefore seems safe to assume also that Jesus, as the eldest child, took over responsibility for the family carpentry business. If true, then Jesus Himself lived part of His life as a saint in the marketplace. During His ministry, He embodied all five of the leadership ministries,

---

40   Our word "ecclesiastic," meaning "of the church," is from the Greek *ecclesia*, which was the main legislative assembly of ancient Athens. Thus, it carries the connotations of rulership and dominion, which when exercised in love are apostolic characteristics. Sadly, the modern Christian church is largely too pastoral and not apostolic enough. Most of its leaders are called "pastors" and as a result their focus is on feeding sheep rather than leading and equipping people to bring the Kingdom to earth (See Chapter 10). We've widely missed the mark. However, that is changing at an accelerating rate.

but when He ascended He divided and distributed the five pieces among men. As explained by Dr. Bill Hamon:

"Jesus is the Apostle of the Church, the Prophet, Evangelist, Pastor, and Teacher. Christ was all five of those ministries manifested in one human body. When the body of Jesus...ascended back to the Father, those ministries were then given to certain members of the Corporate Body of Christ."[41]

Jesus' followers became sons of God, friends of Jesus, and privy to His plans, including the five-fold ministry plan that the apostle Paul summarized and explained for the first time in Ephesians 4:11–16. And many, as we know, became five-fold ministers.

DID IT WORK?

A good question at this point would be, "Does this plan work? Do we have any evidence to point to?"

There is no doubt about it! Somehow, this plan has been the underpinning for the spread of Christianity, or the church, from 12 mostly uneducated men in the 1st Century whose leader was crucified, to the largest religion in the world, lasting 2,000 years, with 2.2 billion believers, and still growing. I'm not saying The Five-fold Effect of Ephesians 4:11–16 is the only reason for this success, but I think it must have had a lot to do with it.

In the next chapter I want us to spend a little more time in relatively familiar surroundings before jumping into what five-fold looks like in the marketplace. Let's see what it looks like, or should look like, in a church setting, which is where it started.

---

41   *Ibid.*, p. 172.

ACTIVATION EXERCISES

1. Were you at all familiar with Ephesians 4:11–16 before reading this book? Had you thought about it in the way that's outlined here, or is this a new way of looking at it for you? If it's new, what is your reaction? Does it make sense, and is it believable?

2. Have you begun to think of yourself in any of the five-fold roles? You probably couldn't help it as you read. On a piece of paper or in the space below, write down your first impression of what your primary five-fold gifting might be. Then keep thinking about it, asking God for guidance, but don't pigeonhole yourself just yet. Read on.

CHAPTER 5

WHAT DOES FIVE-FOLD LEADERSHIP LOOK LIKE IN A CHURCH SETTING?

Before getting further into how five-fold applies to the marketplace, it will be instructive to see what it is supposed to look like in the church. The church is where it started and should therefore be the example for the marketplace.

I describe it this way:

It is a body led by elders representing each of the five-fold gifts and under the authority of a leader with apostolic gifting. These leaders train and equip others to operate in these five and other gifts in order to work together perfectly, by the power of the Holy Spirit, so that the church accomplishes its mission, whatever that mission might be.

The elders may or may not have titles, although typically the apostolic leader might be called the "pastor" (even though this is a misnomer as we'll see in Chapter 10). Some of the elders may actually hold conferred titles, which could be "elder," "deacon," or some other title indicating their place in the official hierarchy according to the particular form of government being used. Others may be "elders in fact," men and women who because of their spiritual maturity and skill in their giftings are seen by others as leaders. Each of these people may operate in more than one gift, but one gift usually predominates. Together these form a leadership team which may be large or small, or sometimes teams within a team, and they understand that their role is to equip the other members of the body to do the work the Lord has called them to do as individuals and as a body.[42]

The prophetically gifted leaders, the pastorally gifted, the teachers, and the evangelists on the team each have specific roles and responsibilities to the team and to the body, which we will examine more closely later, especially in Chapters 9 and 10.[43] Simplistically put, all five are to work together in other-centered love to train others in their gifts so that the grass roots ministry of the body can fulfill God's purposes for it. This is what is meant by "to prepare God's people" (NIV) or "for the perfecting of the saints" (KJV), more popularly stated as *equipping* the saints. In so doing, and this is important, they are also responsible to help discern the destiny, i.e., God's purpose and calling, of each person in the organization and help them to walk in it. (For more on this see Chapter 14)

Here is the simple representation of this concept again, but be aware that while there is only one apostle, i.e., one main leader, there is room for more than one of each of the other five in any given church body. (There may be other apostolic people in the body too, but still only the one who is the apostle over it.)

---

42   For more on this, see *How to Build a Winning Team* by Mark and Patti Virkler, Communion with God Ministries, Cheektowaga, NY.

43   An excellent and eye-opening (for me) discussion of this is found in Graham Cooke's previously cited book, *A Divine Confrontation: Birth Pangs of the New Church*, © 1999, Destiny Image Publishers, Inc., Shippensburg, PA, 2001 printing, pp. 6–18.

Figure 5–1: Five-Fold Leadership Model for Church

The resulting "...whole body, joined and knit together... by which every part does its share...causes growth of the body" (Ephesians 4:16), describes a fully functioning, well coordinated organization, every member of which is perfectly placed and equipped to do, and is doing, needed jobs that perfectly contribute to the success of the enterprise.

ARE YOU IN AN "APOSTOLIC" CHURCH?

If you can describe the workings of your church and its leadership as similar to this, you are in a five-fold ministry, or apostolic, church. In this context the word "apostolic" doesn't just mean "apostle-like." As does Graham Cooke, we can use the term "apostolic," or "apostolic practice," when referring to the five-fold ministries operating together in the life of a church.[44]

This presupposes no particular official form of church government, nor am I espousing any. All of them have their inherent strengths and weaknesses, and it is not my intention to delve very far into that except to assert that the five-fold ministry principles can work in any of them. Nor do you have to change the

---

44   *Ibid.*, p.6.

official governmental structure of your church in order to become an apostolic church. The principles are "extra-organizational."

GRACE CHURCH AS AN EXAMPLE OF APOSTOLIC PRACTICE

Remember my description in Chapter 1 of the transformation taking place at Grace Church in High Point, North Carolina? I'm not saying Grace is better than your church or any other. Every church is different, and its governance, organization and operations should be led by God, so don't take Grace as a model for how your church or any other should look. I offer it here as merely an example of an apostolic church, although a good one.

Grace Church is independent and non-denominational (but such independence is not a prerequisite to being apostolic). Its governing structure is similar to the typical Presbyterian form of government, but less formal. There is a "Leadership Council" roughly corresponding to a Presbyterian Session, made up of the pastors, elders and deacons. The Council's stated objective is: "Seeking God together under the leadership of the Holy Spirit with Christ as head of the church to achieve the spiritual and practical objectives that are on His heart for the body at Grace."

"A general consensus" of the Council decides matters affecting the life of the church. If no consensus can be reached by the Council, then a matter is decided by the elders.

The system of checks and balances in this form of government allows for apostolic leadership, but it doesn't call for it. In many such churches a strong leader, usually the senior pastor, does take charge and is deferred to by the staff and the elders either by force of personality or just because that's the traditional, conventional and accepted "way things have always been done." Such deference is often not conducive to the healthiest of leadership practices, however, especially if the senior pastor governs by fiat like a typical company CEO.

On the other hand, if there is no such deference because there are strong personalities on the staff and board, there can be a power struggle with results that are tantamount to a leadership vacuum, with no one clearly exercising apostolic authority. I have witnessed this situation in churches. The politics eventually become overwhelming, quenching much of what the Holy Spirit might want to do there.

By contrast, Rodney Odom is recognized as *the* apostolic leader at Grace Church, although not the only apostolic person there. Exercising his apostolic gift and with the establishing of The 411 Group, wise use of the Leadership Council, and the fostering of an environment of freedom and safety, he has crafted an approach that rises above the often constraining and Holy Spirit quenching results of power struggles or too much structure.

WE DO NEED STRUCTURE

It's not that there is no need for structure. Clearly the Bible, while never prescribing any particular form of church government in the New Testament, does indicate through its references to the appointment of elders in various churches that at least some rudimentary structure is needed and desirable. See Acts 11:30 and 14:23, 1 Timothy 5:7, and Titus 1:5 where elders were appointed under apostolic authority. Many other references to elders are found in the New Testament, but it is not clear whether these were appointed or simply recognized as such because of their following as leaders.

Several passages in the Book of Acts refer to the church headquartered in Jerusalem and the local churches as being led by "apostles and elders," clearly marking a distinction between them or at least indicating that not all elders were apostles. The New Testament term "elder," while it has a meaning close to that of "shepherd," emphasizing pastoral characteristics, allows for a much broader definition of "caring for the flock," which includes teaching and the prophetic as well. In Acts 13:1–3 we see that there were prophets and teachers among the elders in the church at Antioch, along with apostles Barnabas and Saul (later called Paul). No doubt there were elders with evangelistic and other gifts, as well as pastoral.

Regardless of structure, they were already learning to operate according to God's plan of governance which Paul described fully in Ephesians 4:11–16.[45] *Again, the point is, the legal or "official" governmental structure doesn't matter. The principles can be applied to any and all.* They serve the main end, which is to grow the Kingdom.

A WORD ABOUT ADMINISTRATION

Sometimes viewed as a dirty word, administration is actually one of the gifts listed in 1 Corinthians 12:28,[46] right up there with the "big" ones and in fact ahead of speaking in tongues (which is what some people think administrative folks do anyway just to confuse them). But where does administration fit in?

While I was working on a church long-range plan some years ago, God showed me the purpose of administration:

Administration is to support the mission by facilitating an environment where ministries are performed effectively with a minimum of distraction, individuals can receive ministry appropriate for their needs and place in their walk with Christ, and optimal stewardship can be exercised

---

45   It would be interesting to know the leadership structure of the church at Ephesus, since that is the church Paul was writing to when he laid out the five-fold plan in Ephesians 4:11–16. However, maybe it's just as well we don't know much about it or we might slavishly try to copy it.

46   "And in the church God has appointed first of all apostles, second prophets, third teachers, then workers of miracles, also those having gifts of healing, those able to help others, those with gifts of administration, and those speaking in different kinds of tongues."

over the resources entrusted by the Lord to the church. In addition, Administration seeks to glorify God through the practice of excellence in the administrative functions themselves.

Central to this purpose is the idea of allowing the leadership, ministers (the people), and staff to focus on development and execution of their ministries by relying for administrative support on people best equipped to provide it.

In other words, administration keeps the back room stuff from getting in the way of the ministry (or the workplace tasks) and in so doing is a ministry in itself. Apart from being on staff as administrators, people with administrative and organizational gifts have valuable roles. They may help organize volunteer events, assist in planning the launch of new ministries or the maintenance of existing ones, write reports for the church Website, or any number of things that require the sifting and sorting of multiple moving parts into some kind of order.

All of that sounds pretty important to me, yet it is but one part of the "whole body, joined and held together by every supporting ligament."

ACTIVATION EXERCISES

1. Think about your church. Would you describe it as a five-fold, or apostolic, church in terms of its leadership and governance? If your answer is yes, why do you say that? Be specific and make a list of the characteristics you see that make it apostolic.

2. Having listed the characteristics, do you still think your church is apostolic? If not, or maybe somewhat but not entirely, what five-fold gifts, characteristics, traits, or practices seem to be missing?

3. Pray and ask God to show you if there is some role He would like you to play in helping your church become more apostolic, assuming you want it to be.

CHAPTER 6

TRANSITION TO THE MARKETPLACE

I realize I have been using the terms apostle, prophet, evangelist, pastor and teacher as if everyone has a perfect understanding of what they mean. I think most people do have an understanding of these terms sufficient for the conversation we've been having so far. We will look at each one in more detail, but first I want to segue from church to marketplace by pointing out the parallels between each of these offices or giftings and their so-called secular counterparts.

Many non-church organizations, including businesses, already apply some Ephesians 4 principles in the way they are organized and staffed, but usually without knowing they are from the Bible. To illustrate this, we can look at Ephesians 4:11–16 again as if it is about a business organization instead of only the church.

What are the gifts and roles often seen in business organizations?

- a <u>vision caster</u>, often the CEO, who faithfully keeps the organization focused on its mission (<u>apostolic</u>)
- people with <u>foresight</u> and a sense of timing to see

opportunities, marketplace needs, and potential pitfalls; advise the leadership; analyze situations; call attention to problems; encourage and exhort; create and develop; such as marketing or financial managers and strategic planners (prophetic)

- people who win friends and create the means for growth, such as sales people, recruiters, marketers, and PR people who spread the good news about the company (evangelistic)
- people who have compassion for those struggling to find their place, such as HR people, coaches, ombudsmen, or even outplacement people (pastoral)
- people who understand the vision and can explain and translate it for others into practical action in each functional area, such as managers and trainers (teaching)

It is no accident that these functions roughly correspond to the five-fold gifts plus the gifts of service and administration. For one thing, if you believe these gifts *are* found among people in the church (and I suppose you do by now or you probably wouldn't be this far along in the book), why would you think the people would lose their gifts when they step out the door into the church parking lot?

(By the way, the products and services of the business may be the "signs and wonders," calling attention to the quality and power of the company just as healings, miracles, and prophecy call attention to the glory of God!)

SPIRIT AND AUTHORITY

At Pentecost, the apostle Peter reminded everyone that the Spirit is poured out on *all* people (Acts 2:17a). This is seen in the creativity, talents and aptitudes (gifts) of believers and non-believers alike, including the supernatural gifts of the Spirit (1 Cor.

12:27–31, Rom. 12:4–8 and Ephesians 4:11. Also see Matthew 5:45b[47]). Therefore, everyone has one or more of these gifts, and the only requirement is that people operate in roles suitable to their gifts and to their calling. It should be no surprise, then, that the five-fold functions are found in the marketplace.

We also know that all authority comes from God, even the authority of people we may not like or agree with.[48] Jesus never challenged the authority of Caesar, Herod or the Pharisees. In fact, he showed respect for it. When He criticized, it was their actions he was addressing.

With that in mind, let's have some fun. Let's take the liberty of paraphrasing Ephesians 4:11–16 as if it had been written about a business:

> And He Himself gave some to be CEOs and department heads, some strategic planners and financial managers, some salesmen and public relations people, and some human resources people and trainers, for the equipping of the employees to do the work of the company, for the growth and profitability of the company and the benefit of all its stakeholders, till we all come to a unity of understanding the company's values and goals and of the knowledge that the company's mission and the authority to carry it out were provided by the Son of God, until everybody is perfectly placed to do, and is doing, a needed job that perfectly contributes to the success of the enterprise just as Christ perfectly fulfilled his mission on earth;
>
> that we should no longer be aimless recruits, tossed to and fro and carried about with every wind of rumor and

---

47   "for he maketh his sun to rise on the evil and on the good, and sendeth rain on the just and on the unjust." (KJV)

48   Romans 13:1–7, respecting those in authority because it is God-given; Ephesians 6:5–9 (and elsewhere), serving as if you were serving the Lord.

poor training, by the trickery of men who have their own agendas, in the cunning craftiness of deceitful plotting and office politics or the saying of, "that's the way we've always done it," but, speaking the truth in love, may grow up in all ways into the company He has destined it to be, with Him as the head—Christ—from whom the whole organization, joined and knit together by what every person and part supplies, according to the effective working by which every part does its share, causes growth of the company for its profitability, which we love (WPV).[49]

We can laugh, but these are more than just secular parallels. They are the real thing.

Figure 6–1 takes the five-fold gifts and relates them to some of the positions in a company where the indicated characteristics are often found. This is a universal model for organizational formation. I'll develop this idea more between here and Chapter 10.

Figure 6–1: Universal Five-Fold Leadership Model for Business (Position Examples)

---

49   Walt Pilcher Version

THE IMPACT OF APOSTOLIC LEADERSHIP IN THE MARKETPLACE

In *Good to Great,* author Jim Collins studied 28 well-known companies, 11 of which started from an observable transition point and over a 15 year period greatly outperformed their markets. The 11 were compared to a carefully selected set of companies in the same industries that did not show a leap to greatness.

The question was, "What did the good-to-great companies share in common *that distinguished them from the comparison companies?*"[50] The main finding identified the CEOs of these companies as what Collins called "Level 5 leaders." Surprisingly, **what the Level 5 leaders had in common were what we would call apostolic characteristics**, unlike those of their domineering CEO counterparts in less successful companies.

- The Level 5 leader "builds enduring greatness through a paradoxical blend of personal humility and professional will."[51]
- Having egos and great ambition, but foremost for the institution, not themselves
- Humble and modest, never boastful, yet fearless. Seemingly ordinary people quietly producing extraordinary results.
- Workmanlike diligence—more plow horse than show horse
- Unwavering resolve to do what must be done
- Setting the tone; motivating by inspired standards, not personal charisma
- Driven to produce results, to build a great company no matter how difficult
- Setting up successors for success, even at personal sacrifice

---

50 *Op. cit.,* p. 7, italics added.

51 *Ibid.,* p. 20.

- Giving credit to others when things go well; taking responsibility when they don't

Compare this list to any list of apostolic characteristics, such as those coming up in Chapters 9 and 10, and you will see there are striking similarities.

In addition,

- The Level 5 leader gets the "right people on the bus" (and the wrong people off) even before figuring out where to drive it, believing that once this is done then vision and direction for the company will come through the talent and inspiration of the people remaining.
- The Level 5 leader fosters a culture of discipline combined with an ethic of entrepreneurship.

These company leaders took great care in selecting, grooming and equipping the right people for the right jobs, just as in a five-fold leadership organization.

The 11 companies were very successful, way more successful than their peer companies, most of which would themselves also be considered successful. Remember, these 11 were not thinking in terms of a complete version of the five-fold leadership model, yet they applied an effective form of it. We do not know how many of the leaders were intentionally hearing and being led and empowered by the Holy Spirit, but it is probably safe to assume most were not. Even so, The Five-fold Effect can be seen.

That leads right into the next chapter, the main thesis of this book.

ACTIVATION EXERCISES

1. Do you see the parallels between the five-fold gifts and traditional business functions? What, if anything, surprises you about this? Do you think the argument here is valid, or is it too much of a stretch, a case of overworking an analogy? If the latter, why?

2. As you read about the parallels, and about the "Level 5 leaders," did any specific people you know come to mind that seem to fit the roles listed? Did you see yourself in any of them?

CHAPTER 7

World-Changing Implications – The Main Thesis

The "Theory of the Case"

The arguments presented so far can be summarized and used to construct a succinct "theory of the case" for why the Ephesians 4 model applies to all organizations.

1. God provided the five-fold ministry and the gifts to support it for the effective transformational leadership of the church, both the church at large and the local church. To work best, it requires empowerment by the Holy Spirit.

2. The church and society (marketplace) are inseparable, and so the equipping of the saints (believers) is to better prepare them to serve in church and the marketplace so that their organizations are built up for the glory of God.

3. The Spirit is poured out on *all* flesh (Acts 2:17–18) and is manifested in creativity, talents and aptitudes (gifts) of believers and non-believers alike.

4. The result, or fruit, of this pouring out will be more apparent or stronger in believers, who have the Spirit indwelling as well as having an "innate" (from having been born again) and cultivatable understanding of the purposes and power of the Holy Spirit and how to operate in the gifts, than in non-believers, who do not (John 14:12–14).[52]

5. Therefore, the five-fold ministry model is as applicable to non-church organizations, e.g., businesses, clubs, homeowners associations, committees, etc., as it is to churches and para-church organizations.

6. Organizations applying the model, even if they are run by non-believers, will be more successful than organizations that do not apply the model, because it is God's model.

7. Organizations populated by believers applying the model will be much more successful than both non-believer organizations and believer organizations not applying the model because of their greater and potentially unlimited ability to operate in the power of the Holy Spirit (again, John 14:12–14).

As we saw previously, when we talk about the "saints" being equipped "for the works of the ministry," or "works of service," we are talking about all believers doing whatever they do in any kind of service to others, whether in church on Sunday or outside of it during the week. As Dr. C. Peter Wagner says:

"What we do in the workplace Monday through Saturday is true ministry. Believers who are bus drivers or farmers

---

52 "I tell you the truth, anyone who has faith in me will do what I have been doing. He will do even greater things than these, because I am going to the Father. And I will do whatever you ask in my name, so that the Son may bring glory to the Father. You may ask me for anything in my name, and I will do it." (John 14:12–14)

or corporate CEOs or electricians or television producers or elected government officials or school teachers or stay-at-home moms or newspaper reporters are all doing ministry."[53]

Non-believers are included in this, even though it is not correct to call them "saints." "Pre-saints" maybe.

EVERYONE HAS A MINISTRY

Everyone, believer or non-believer, has a ministry[54] when he or she performs services for others. So, right now, Saint Walt is writing this book as a service to many. Saint Todd (my son, an attorney) is helping clients with immigration or political asylum issues. Saint Cecelia (a friend) is helping business owners plan the most efficient use of their office space. And Saint Graham Cooke is speaking words of life to strangers at his favorite purveyor of legal stimulants, which he likes to call St. Arbucks.

CHURCH UNIVERSAL, LOCAL CHURCH (OR PARA-CHURCH), AND MARKETPLACE ORGANIZATIONS

I've been throwing around terms like "the church," "church," "para-church," and "marketplace" as types of organizations. Since that may be confusing, I'd like to clarify by describing what I'll

---

53   Wagner, *The Church in the Workplace*, p. 108

54   Interestingly, although we don't do it in the United States, many countries call their government agencies "ministries." In England, politicians holding office are called "ministers," from the same Latin word which means "servant," starting with the chief government official, the Prime Minister. It is not uncommon to find in many countries a Ministry of Defense or a Ministry of Education, to name only two. (And let us not forget Monty Python's indispensable Ministry of Silly Walks.)

call Three Stages of Revelation about the purpose and scope of five-fold ministry leadership.

STAGE 1 – THE TRADITIONAL VIEW: JUST FOR CHURCH WORK

This view encompasses only the church universal (the whole body of Christ worldwide) and the local, individual church or para-church organization, and it touches only lightly on the world or marketplace. For simplicity's sake I'll ignore the role of denominational hierarchies, networks, and other forms of affiliation. In this Stage 1 view, the church is governed by high level apostles, prophets, evangelists, pastors and teachers who equip others to govern the local, individual congregations or para-church organizations, and they appoint such people to be five-fold ministers to lead these bodies. The church and the churches touch the marketplace mainly to the extent of performing charitable services, funding and populating missionary work (which is really just an extension of church), new church planting, and exhorting their members to live their weekday lives as Christian witnesses to the world so that more people will become Christians.

That's all good, but evangelistically it's fairly passive in terms of outreach and impact. Fortunately, this view has largely given way to a wider one, Stage 2, below.

STAGE 2 – EQUIPPING FOR WORKS OF SERVICE IN THE MARKETPLACE, NOT JUST THE CHURCH

This view takes things a big step further and recognizes that Christians not only need to be good witnesses and examples by the way they live their lives, but also they need to be marketplace ministers. This is about truly tearing down the walls between the church and the community. In other words, Christians are to view themselves as servant leaders and their work as acts of loving service to others and "as unto the Lord" (Ephesians 6:7).

They are to take to the marketplace those ministries traditionally reserved for church or the hospital or other traditionally "safe" or "appropriate" places. These include such services as praying for the sick for physical and inner healing and deliverance, prophesying, organizing prayer meetings or Bible studies at work or in the home for people outside their churches, Christian counseling and coaching, volunteering for civic duties, and/or establishing facilities or resources for marketplace people who want biblically based advice about practical problems and opportunities. Many of these activities traditionally reserved for church or hospital visits can and should as easily be done at the mall. Along the way, Christians should be tithing, supporting charities, doing good deeds, and tipping generously.

Furthermore, they are encouraged, if not really trained (although there are many good books on this), to apply Kingdom principles in their businesses. However, this is usually without reference to five-fold leadership.

Some may find themselves with opportunities to prophesy, witness and evangelize to major leaders in government, business, and the other five mountains, including religion.

Thus, the impact on the marketplace is more than tangential and can actually change people's and communities' lives in ways beyond a charitable handout or a Christian lifestyle witness (though I am not at all downplaying the potential impact of a salvation testimony). The church is out in the world, not waiting for the world to come to church.

But even this is not enough. It falls short of God's plan to restore Eden to Earth by fulfilling our Genesis call to take dominion over the planet. Churches still tend to envision results more in terms of programs, structures, and how many seats are filled and less in terms of a way of life in the presence of God that helps fulfill His Kingdom purpose. We must change this.

STAGE 3 – FIVE-FOLD, FIVE-FOLD EVERYWHERE

This revolutionary way of looking at things goes two steps further. With Stage 2 as a given, it first recognizes that to implement Stage 2 best, five-fold leadership is to be modeled and taught in the church and in churches. The second and last step to Stage 3 is when five-fold is established at every level of every organization, whether a church denomination, a local church, a para-church organization, or one in the marketplace. Stage 3 more fully recognizes and lives out the fact that there is no separation between church and marketplace. (Recall Deuteronomy 16:13–17 and Zechariah 2 from Chapters 2 and 3.)

It is the church's responsibility to get this ball rolling faster, and the sooner the better. It starts with you and me because we are the church.

THE REFINED THESIS

Below, I show the theory boiled down to the two-part thesis we first saw in the Introduction. Here is why understanding and applying the five-fold ministry paradigm can be world-changing. Think of it as two levels of potential organizational effectiveness:

Level 1
Teams of leaders with complementary gift sets corresponding to the five-fold gifts of the Spirit (as well as the motivational gifts[55]) will create organizations that are more successful than those not led in that way because working together in concert and alignment is more efficient than working alone or at cross purposes.[56]

---

55   Romans 12:3–8: Perceiving, serving, teaching, encouraging, giving, ruling, mercy. More about this in Chapter 11.

56   "In the multitude of counselors there is safety" (Prov. 11:14) and "…a threefold cord is not easily broken" (Ecclesiastes 4:12)

Level 2

Organizations that not only employ the paradigm above, but also are led by people who have a relationship with Jesus and an indwelling of the Holy Spirit, combined with an understanding of how to be led by Him in the exercise of their Holy Spirit-given gifts, will operate in much more power, supernatural power, in fact, and therefore enjoy much more effectiveness and success than will those that do not.

BE A CHANGE-MAKER

Either level is desirable and is more effective than the way most organizations are currently led. But just imagine how much better Level 2 can be because it relies on and receives supernatural help!

Later on, I'll give some illustrations or examples of what it looks like when organizations operate according to these paradigms, especially Level 2. Also, be assured that even if you do not work in an organization that is run this way, and even if you do not have the authority or influence to change that, you can still have a five-fold impact on it. This, too, will be covered more fully later.

Keep in mind, the world is changing fast. I've heard it said that we've seen more change in the past 30 years than civilization has seen in the past 30 centuries. Change is happening at an accelerating rate. We are hurtling toward God knows where. And that's the point: God does know where, and He's willing to share as much about that as we need to know. We need much more than simple agility to keep up, even if that agility is computer assisted. Rather than continuing to be reactive and responsive to changes that have already occurred or that we have to essentially guess at, we need supernatural help not only to keep up, but also to anticipate and prepare for the future before it happens. We need to be more than what the world likes to call "proactive."

Supernatural help is available through disciplined application of the five-fold ministry and leadership gifts He gave us. Think of it as being proactive on steroids. With this, you and your organization can not only be ready for the changes that are coming, but can also be change-makers. Organizations without this are ill-equipped to face the future.

SUPERNATURAL LEADERSHIP

What we are talking about here is supernatural leadership. We would expect that to be more powerful and effective than natural leadership, wouldn't we? There is no limit to the Holy Spirit's power working through us except whatever limit we ourselves impose by fear and unbelief. If you are still skeptical, then just go with me here based on asking again, "What if it's true?"

Max Myers in his book *The Tail that Wags the Dog*, contrasts natural leadership with supernatural leadership.[57] See which one you think would be the more powerful.

1. Natural leadership depends on my efforts. Supernatural leadership depends on God for the results.

2. Natural leadership depends on hard work and development of skills. Supernatural leadership depends on the person's willingness to listen to and follow Father God.

3. Natural leadership is a model that depends on the performance of others. Supernatural leadership's focus is on relationships that set people free to use their gifts.

4. Natural leadership, with its systems, often places leaders in a place of being controlled by others. Supernatural leadership allows the leader to be free of control or manipulation of others.

5. Natural leadership expects leaders to do the "dirty work"

---

57   Max J. Myers, *The Tail that Wags the Dog*, Creation House, a Strang Company, © 2009, pp. 66–73.

for those they lead. Supernatural leadership points people to personal responsibility.

6. Natural leadership is dependent upon intelligence and education. Supernatural leadership requires an inner brilliance.

Max explains these points in helpful detail, and I recommend you read his eye-opening book. He is not at all suggesting that there is a substitute for hard work, sacrifice, development of skills, and respect for authority or others on the team. He is saying we aren't to *depend* on those factors ahead of depending on the Holy Spirit's empowerment that makes all of those most effective and timely. In the supernatural five-fold leadership plan, the Holy Spirit is allowed to orchestrate the activities that put into effect Ephesians 4:14–16:

"Then we will no longer be infants, tossed back and forth by the waves, and blown here and there by every wind of teaching and by the cunning and craftiness of men in their deceitful scheming. Instead, speaking the truth in love, we will in all things grow up into him who is the Head, that is, Christ. From him the whole body, joined and held together by every supporting ligament, grows and builds itself up in love, as each part does its work."

WHAT IF, INDEED?

In the Introduction I posed several tantalizing "what if?" questions:

What if there is a way to assure your organization will enjoy the favor of God, be a blessing all those who come in contact with it, and be the most effective, powerful and successful organization ever?

What if God has a plan for how things should operate in the marketplace and you can tap into it? What if instead of using the world's poor imitation of this plan, you can use the real thing? What if you apply the real plan to your life in the marketplace, and what if in so doing you could position your organization for whatever the future holds?

Here's another "what if." What if all the world's businesses, institutions and organizations practiced apostolic five-fold leadership? If extraordinary became the norm? I think the five-fold paradigm should be taught in seminaries, schools of ministry, Bible colleges, and business schools at both the undergraduate and the graduate level worldwide so that we can more rapidly move toward it becoming the norm.

Are you beginning to see the potential of this? I wish I could quantify for you what your results will be, but I believe God has guaranteed through His promise when giving us the five-fold gifts that there will be results and that they will be stunning. All you have to do for a start is to be "good soil" for these ideas to be planted in, remembering the parable related in Matthew: "Still other seed fell on good soil, where it produced a crop—a hundred, sixty or thirty times what was sown" (Matthew 13:8).

Your success will be a beacon pointing to God's glory. When people come to you and ask, "How did you do it?" what a great opportunity for evangelism you will have!

I hope you are beginning to ask, "Okay, what should I do?" Before answering that, I want to share the story of a business venture embarked upon *without* the benefit of the theoretical foundation you now have. It's fiction, but is it really?

ACTIVATION EXERCISES

1. Does this make sense to you? Have you ever thought about it this way, or is this truly a new way of thinking for you? Does it give you a sense of excitement?

2. Discuss this chapter (theory and thesis) with at least two people. Does it make sense to them, whether they believe it or not? Are they excited about it? Do they have their own copies of the book by now?

3. By yourself, or in the discussion with your two friends, make a list of three or four implications this may have for you. In other words, list some things you might want to do differently as a result of this new way of thinking.

4. Would you rather your organization operate at Level 1 effectiveness, or Level 2?

CHAPTER 8

"Not so Good, Not so Great"

A Cautionary tale

Fred was beside himself with excitement as he pulled into his garage and ran to the kitchen to greet his wife.

"Judy, I found it! It's perfect!" he almost shouted.

"What is?" she answered, calmly replacing a dishtowel in its rack under the sink. She was used to Fred's enthusiasm. She reached up and gave him a light kiss. "And good evening to you, too."

"The location for our store. It's perfect, and it's affordable." He paced back and forth in the small kitchen, causing Judy to dodge this way and that to avoid a collision. It was a familiar dance.

"Tell me about it."

Fred had been a senior machinist at a manufacturing plant in town. He was the best, supervising a crew of three, tackling even the most challenging assignments to build, remodel or repair everything from the smallest to the largest of the equipment. Fearless in company lore, he was renowned for crawling into an empty boiler one day to weld a seam without waiting for the rest of his crew to "spot" him or engaging the lockout/tagout safety system. "It just needed to be done," he said. Production was uninterrupted and the company didn't miss its delivery date.

Alas, after 25 years, Fred's job was exported to China without Fred, and he was forced to take early retirement. It was an attractive severance and retirement package, however, and Fred chose to take it as a lump sum. He'd always dreamed of being his own boss, and he would use the money to start a business.

"It's right at the corner of Baker Boulevard and 13th Street. You know how busy that intersection is."

"It's pretty busy all right," agreed Judy. She poured lemonade and set it on the table.

"That means lots of traffic. Just what we'll need for a retail store. And there's a McDonald's on the opposite corner and a gas station across the street. Oh, and an auto parts store right next door. Here's the best part. Since the building's been vacant for over a year, I negotiated a really sweet lease-to-buy deal even though I had to commit to a two-year lease."

Judy sat down at the table which was already set for dinner. "How many parking spaces does it have? How easy is it to get in and out of the lot, especially during rush hour?"

"Not a lot of spaces, but, heck, nobody's going to park longer than it takes to run in, buy a bunch of your cupcakes, and run out, right?"

"I guess not."

Judy's cupcakes were legendary. There were several kinds, most from old family recipes she'd tweaked to fit modern ingredients and ovens. She was always experimenting to make them even better. They were a sure fire hit at the church covered dish suppers, especially among the children, and her neighbors and her five grandchildren were always grateful for a supply. What better idea for a business than to sell "Miss Judy's Own Olde Tyme Recipe" cupcakes? They'd open a store and call it "CupKake City." Fred's idea. "Kind of cute with the 'K,' don't you think?" he had announced. "The ladies will like that." They'd have a "Grande Opening" too. Fred thought fake archaic spelling was classy.

"Not only that," Fred continued, "but the furniture and fixtures and stuff from the previous tenant are still there, and they're ours for no extra charge. We'll have to clean them up and rearrange things a little, but I can do that. It'll be great."

"If you say so."

"Right. How many cupcakes do you think you can make every day? I think I've figured out how many we need to sell to break even." He gave her a number and took his place at the head of the table.

"I can make a lot more than that," she said. The timer on the oven chimed, and Judy rose to fill their plates with pizza. "So how much time do we have to think about this?" she asked as she sat back down.

"Honey, it's a done deal. We can move in next week!"

"You're kidding! Couldn't we talk about this first?"

"That's what we're doing isn't it? Talking about it? Hey, I had to strike while the iron was hot!"

There wasn't much more talk over dinner.

CupKake City opened a month later. It had taken a lot of hard work to get the place ready and more time and money than they'd planned, but Fred was elated. He felt the "Baker" Boulevard address was a good omen. The kitchen was spotless. The fixtures and equipment gleamed. Everything worked flawlessly, from the mixing machines to the air conditioner to the cash register, and even to the napkin dispensers.

"The floor is so clean you could eat off it!" he declared proudly.

Though elated, Fred was exhausted too. At the Grande Opening he was so wired he didn't notice how tired he was, but there was no question the hard work had taken a toll. More than one customer commented about the bags under his eyes, but his cheerful retort was always, "Hey, if you want to talk about bags, here's a bag of Miss Judy's Own Olde Tyme Recipe cupcakes. Take one home! Or two or three!"

And many did. Grande Opening week was a rousing success, cupcakes flying off the shelves. Customers came and went at a furious pace, many commenting on how nice the store looked and how clean it was. Judy had done a good job of decorating when she wasn't toiling over the ovens, although to Fred's eye it seemed like a lot of frou-frou and an unnecessary expense. After the Opening, he'd see that they cut back on some of that.

Their daughter, Kate, who lived several states away with her husband and two toddlers, called Fred and Judy on Grande Opening day.

"Congratulations, you two! I hope all your hard work pays off. I know the cupcakes are good, and if I lived there I'd be your best customer!"

"Thanks, Dear," said Judy.

"Now all you need is to put up a Website and get on Facebook!"

"Haven't got time for that, Kate," said Fred. "Besides, Facebook is just for kids isn't it? Not our kind of customers."

For the next several weeks business was brisk as more and more people tried the new cupcake store, which was sort of a novelty in town. "It's important to be unique and distinctive," Fred said, and it looked like he was right. There were radio and TV spots, large ads and flyers with coupons in the paper, and even a billboard a block away on busy 13th Street with a big arrow pointing toward the store. He had given the advertising agency explicit directions about what he wanted, and they had come through. During the first weekend, Fred had hired some high school kids to stand on Baker Boulevard outside the store in cupcake costumes waving signs and handing out balloons. It had taken a large portion of their money to do all this advertising and promoting, but it seemed to be working. Fred knew the customers would return with repeat business even after the advertising stopped, and tell all their friends, because the cupcakes were that good. CupKake City was off to a great start.

Making sure the cupcakes were good had been the hardest part. Fred spent a long time deciding which of Judy's recipes to include on the menu, rejecting two or three types that Judy liked and replacing them with those he thought would sell better. Judy chafed a little at that but managed to get past it. "Just tell me what to make, and I'll make it," became her *modus operandi*. She was too busy and too tired to argue. What really made it tougher on her was when Fred, shopping for the best deals on bulk ingredients, made little substitutions here and there that affected her results in unexpected ways. A lot of free cupcakes went to charity because of that. "But it's a deductible expense," said Fred, "and we're saving more up front."

One evening as they were cleaning up after closing, Julius, the college student who worked the cash register part time, had an idea. "There's room for two or three tables and chairs. Why not let people sit here and eat their cupcakes instead of having only take-out? And maybe serve coffee or something too."

Judy thought it was a great plan.

"I don't think so," said Fred. "But thanks for the idea. We've got to remember, CupKake City is about cupcakes, not coffee and doughnuts. And if we have people sitting in here with their cars parked too long out there, we'd have a real mess on our hands. It's hard enough to get in and out as it is with all the traffic on Baker Boulevard, and if the parking spills over to the auto parts store the guys there won't like it."

"You could give them free cupcakes," Julius persisted halfheartedly.

"Maybe, but I don't know how long we could afford that."

"Why couldn't we just give them some of the ones we're now giving to charity?" suggested Judy.

"No, they'd know they were getting second best," said Fred.

"Can I tell you something else?" asked Julius.

"Shoot."

"Well, lately a few of the customers have been complaining that the cupcakes they bought this week tasted different from those they bought last week. Like, 'I bought chocolate with sprinkles last week, and it was better than the chocolate with sprinkles I bought this week.' Or sometimes, 'It's better this week.'"

"Pretty fickle if you ask me. Judy, is there anything wrong with the chocolate?"

"Not that I know of."

"Chocolate's chocolate, right?" said Fred.

"But it's not just the chocolate ones," said Julius. "Sometimes it's vanilla, sometimes red velvet maybe." Julius shrugged and resumed sweeping the floor.

"What do you tell them, Julius?" asked Fred.

"Oh, I just say Judy's always trying to make things even better all the time. That seems to make them happy."

"Good boy! The customers really like you I've noticed. Some of them even call you by name, and you know a lot of them too. That's good."

"Thanks."

"Now here's what else you should tell them. Tell them to try a different kind once in awhile. Don't stay in a rut. Just because you like chocolate with sprinkles doesn't mean you won't like angel food with marshmallow icing just as well once in awhile. Okay?"

"Okay, will do."

Fred looked at Judy.

"I'll try to do better," she said.

After the first couple of months business had slowed a bit, as might be expected, but it was still enough to pay the bills and put food on the table at home. They weren't putting any money in the bank, however, and Fred began to have nagging doubts about whether they would ever recover the retirement savings and severance they had invested in the business. Still, it was too early to panic. He kept changing the menu to ensure variety and to keep the customers' interest up. One major pain was having to hire and train a succession of cash register clerks to help with sales. Julius had gone off for a semester in Paris, and the other college kids who applied didn't seem interested in working very hard. Some offered suggestions for the business, like Julius had done, but what did they know after all? They came and went, generally not staying long enough to get to know the customers.

Sales continued to slide. There was no money for more advertising unless they dipped into their savings or borrowed from their children. Fred had already talked to the bank and been turned down. It seemed to him that banks only lent money to people who didn't need it.

On a rare afternoon off, Judy joined the "Y" so she could have a place to go for exercise once in awhile. Fred had not encouraged it, even though the expense was small. She did it anyway, and he didn't say much about it after that. As she entered the fitness room and mounted the treadmill, she overheard some other women talking among themselves.

"I'm new in town," one said. "Do you know of any good bakeries?"

"Yeah, there are a few," said another.

"I can tell you one to avoid," said a third.

"Oh yeah, which one?"

"That one that sells cupcakes, over on Baker Boulevard."

"I've been there," said number two. "It was great when it first opened, although the traffic was terrible for getting in and out of the place."

"That's right," said number three. "The cupcakes were good, but then they seemed to keep changing the recipe or something so I stopped going back as much. Then one day the kid behind the counter got a little snotty with me, so I just quit going entirely. It's not worth the hassle. And that name, 'CupKake City,' with a 'K'? It's a little too cutesy for me."

Judy didn't hear the rest of their conversation. She felt like throwing up. She made a hasty exit and went home and crawled into bed, even though it was only mid-afternoon.

That night she told Fred about it.

"It's just gossip girls," he said, dismissing the incident in an effort to reduce Judy's obvious anxiety. "Beside, there's bound to be a few people who don't like something. Never said we could please everybody."

But that night as he tried to fall asleep, Fred had to admit he was troubled, and still very tired.

The days and weeks came and went, as did the customers, and the help, but business was steady if maybe declining little by little. There were encouraging spikes around holidays and when they offered specials, but those were balanced by slow days when it seemed nobody even knew what a cupcake was, much less wanted to buy one.

Then, the unthinkable happened. Fred got sick.

"It's his heart," the doctor told Judy. "He'll live, and we'll probably discharge him in a couple of days, but he won't be able to work for at least eight weeks, and even after that he won't be able to keep up the same pace. He really needs to retire."

"He won't like that," Judy said.

"He won't like the alternative any better."

Judy did the best she could under the circumstances. Fred was home and ambulatory, but he couldn't remember things, couldn't fix his own meals except cereal or a sandwich now and then, and he needed reminding to take his meds. He was angry and depressed all the time. Insurance covered most, but not all, of Fred's medical expenses. The care giving was very wearing on Judy on top of having to run the business almost singlehandedly. Their daughter, Kate, flew in to help right away, but she could only stay a few days before she had to get back to her children.

Fred had never shown Judy the books, and she was appalled

when she saw the financial condition of the company. Caring for Fred, she couldn't spend as much time baking, and she often ran out of cupcakes to sell before the day was over. She cut back the store hours. Without Fred's disciplinary oversight, the hired help became less and less efficient, arriving late, failing to clean up properly, and occasionally giving Judy some lip. She didn't know the suppliers or the deals Fred had worked out so sometimes ingredients and supplies were delivered late, further cutting into production. Some of the suppliers took advantage and raised their prices. As she ordered less and less, the quantity discounts disappeared. Bills were pouring in faster than sales receipts. To top it all off, CupKake City's restaurant sanitation rating slipped from 101.5 to 90, which depressed Fred even more.

By the time Fred recovered it was really too late. There was only one thing to do.

Nine months after its Grande Opening, with 12 months left on its lease, and with Fred's and Judy's money gone, the business closed. CupKake City became a half baked ghost town.

Fred and Judy were the only mourners.

DISCUSSION

What's wrong with this picture? What isn't?! It's a pretty realistic story, I think. Remember to think in terms of the five-fold gifts of apostle, prophet, evangelist, pastor and teacher. Did you see any of them in operation here?

To be fair, there are a few things we can applaud about Fred's performance and behavior, but not many. First, he was completely dedicated to the enterprise, an important apostolic trait. Second, he took upon himself the tasks he was good at, such as preparing and maintaining the machinery and the cleanliness of the facility. He also did a pretty good job of administration, keeping the books and doing the "back room" office work so Judy could focus on what he thought her role should be, which was production, that is, the baking, plus decorating the store, an evangelistic function.

Unfortunately, however, even before the store opened we knew Fred was not a team player but more of a grandstander. Crawling into the boiler without safety protection may have seemed heroic, and it did achieve its purpose, but it was selfish (bringing glory to Fred) and foolish. He should have been cited for it by company management, but either they didn't know all the facts or they chose to ignore them. In any case, it probably served to reinforce the lone wolf behavior he showed with the cupcake store.

So, while Fred was always courteous to Judy and Julius, and he recognized and praised them when he thought their work was good, i.e., up to his standards, he only paid lip service to their attempts to provide input that wasn't in line with his vision. He never really formed them into a team. The "team" was only Fred and some helpers, which is all Judy, Julius and the ad agency really were to him. That is the opposite of five-fold ministry in action. It was always only Fred's vision, not a vision growing out of an idea and then shaped by the team under the leadership of an apostolic figure before being implemented.

Was the prophetic in play here? Judy was perceptive and

discerning and demonstrated foresight when she observed the potential pitfalls of the location and the lease arrangements. But Fred rejected this input. He did the same when Julius had a prophetic/evangelistic suggestion about bringing in tables and chairs. Fred's one, unconscious, nod to the prophetic was seeing the "Baker" Boulevard address as a good omen. Of course, relying on omens is never a good idea.

Except for praising Julius for relating well to the customers, Fred completely took over the evangelistic (sales and marketing) side by himself, despite not having any expertise in it. The ad agency did a good job, but they were just carrying out Fred's plan. There is no evidence Fred asked the agency for their ideas, even though that's what ad agencies do very well. He only wanted to know how much it would cost to implement his own ideas. He was so self-assured, buoyed by the initial success of the store, that he spent almost all his advertising and promotion money up front and failed to keep any in reserve for later use, which the ad agency would have recommended (and maybe did, in vain). He thought Judy spent too much on keeping the store nicely decorated, even though he knew the customers liked it. Even after praising Julius, the next words out of Fred's mouth were to give Julius direction to tell the customers to shape up and essentially do things Fred's way. Not very evangelistic, failing to "meet the customers where they are" the way Jesus did.

Consistent product quality is another very important evangelistic strategy Fred failed to appreciate. Judy might have tried to tell that to Fred, but he beat her down about it and she gave up, retreating to her kitchen to do the best she could with the ingredients and the menu Fred allowed her to have. These responsibilities should have been Judy's all along. At least Fred did have a positive, enthusiastic attitude and "face" when dealing with the customers himself, if only at first. But even that was probably more about making Fred look good than about advancing the interests of the enterprise.

Fred treated everything as a problem, not as an opportunity, from the tables and chairs idea to the treatment of suppliers and employees. His relationships with the latter were "win/lose" propositions and, later, disciplinary problems, completely missing the one as cause and the other as the effect. A little pastoral input might have been helpful in dealing with the succession of hired help, and maybe even the suppliers. We can't blame Fred for not providing it himself as he was clearly not pastorally gifted. But we can fault him for not recognizing the opportunity, if not the need, and for not enlisting Judy for this. Maybe even Julius before he went away.

When Judy, devastated by the comments she overheard at the "Y," tried to tell Fred about it, he dismissed it. In so doing, he disrespected her as a person, disrespected the prophetic-type input she was providing, failed to provide the pastoral response that might have helped heal her emotionally, and, of course, failed to take seriously the implications of the information she reported. Fred's attitude had in fact already provoked her to an act of insubordination, joining the "Y" against his wishes.

The only teacher in the mix was Fred himself, who was a bad one because he never sought the truth, only what he already thought he knew about any given subject. The ad agency, Judy, the suppliers, and even the bank, could have served as teachers for Fred in their various areas of expertise, but he never allowed them to contribute.

There were warning signs, and not just the gossip at the "Y." Fred never had peace about the way things were going. A lack of peace is often a warning sign from the Holy Spirit that things are not right. But Fred never sought help or advice from anyone. As far as we know, he and Judy never prayed about any of this either. Fred took a lot upon himself. He delegated certain tasks, but not the burden of them, because he really didn't trust anyone, even

Judy, to do things right. We don't know if that affected his physical health, but it might have.

When the crunch came and Fred got sick, the house of cards he had constructed came tumbling down. There was no real team to backstop him. Fred was the keeper of all the information and all the rulebooks. Judy and the others knew only their own narrow areas of responsibility and were unprepared to step into the huge gap created by Fred's absence, even though it was temporary. Even in his darkest hour, if we go by what Judy told the doctor about what Fred's attitude would be about his prognosis, Fred never stopped believing in himself. And that, of course, was the problem. It was all about himself.

Could this have been avoided? A lot of things go into the making of a successful business, and I'm not going to predict that if you decide to open a cupcake store you will succeed just because you think you can do a better job than Fred. It is possible that Fred and Judy shouldn't have opened a cupcake store in the first place. It's possible they shouldn't have gone into business at all. They never prayed about it. They never sought counsel about it. They never really "counted the cost"[58] by having a business plan that allowed for their strengths and weaknesses and had built-in contingencies. All they had was some recipes, albeit good ones, a budget, and their time. They, meaning mostly Fred, just did it, because they, meaning mostly Fred, thought it would be a great idea.

There's a better way. To begin to get a better handle on that, let's take a closer look at each of the five-fold leadership gifts, starting with the apostolic.

---

58 "Suppose one of you wants to build a tower. Will he not first sit down and estimate the cost to see if he has enough money to complete it? For if he lays the foundation and is not able to finish it, everyone who sees it will ridicule him, saying, 'This fellow began to build and was not able to finish'" (Luke 14:28–30).

ACTIVATION EXERCISES

1. Can you see yourself in this story? Which character, or characters if there are more than one, can you most closely identify with?

2. What would you do differently if you really were that (those) character(s)?

3. Can you think of people you know who are like some of these characters? What would you say to them to help them, if you think they need help?

CHAPTER 9

WHAT DO APOSTLES LOOK LIKE?

Well, they pretty much look like you and I except they may have big hair.

But seriously, and without the narrow-minded stereotyping, I want to spend a chapter focusing on this foundational gift because it is, well, so foundational. When we refer to "apostolic practice" or "apostolic leadership," we are talking of course not just about apostles. We are describing organizations that understand and employ all of the gifts of the people involved. However, because these are led by apostolic figures, and since you are likely to find yourself in an apostolic role more often than not, even if that is not your primary gifting, it is worth taking some time to focus on the apostle before moving on to the other four.

Graham Cooke gives an excellent description of what apostles are.

"Apostles are *father figures* who *produce quality leaders* who, in turn, nurture and strengthen the flock. They are wise master builders who lay the correct spiritual foundations."[59] They are

---

59   *Ibid,*, p. 7.

vision casters and catalytic leaders. They give identity. They are architects. They set the atmosphere. They shape or restructure the leadership.

What are the characteristics of apostolic people?[60] They:

- Have a heart passion for the whole of the organization, enterprise or endeavor
- Are gifted to lead, organize, develop, build and expand; may have administrative ability or at least an appreciation for it
- May have experience in the other five-fold ministries they oversee
- Are less emotional and more structured
- Want to see things organized and running smoothly
- Want all the gifts to be present in a balanced, effective, life giving way
- Judge others by their ability and willingness to fit in
- Influence people by helping them to see their value and place in the overall picture
- Get everyone working together as a team; good troubleshooters
- Set others up for success, not failure
- Are recognized more for the fruit of what is produced than for a title

Finally, apostles are servant leaders with the heart of a father, not a stereotypical domineering CEO. They have great authority, but domination is forbidden of leaders in the Kingdom:

"Jesus called them together and said, 'You know that the rulers of the Gentiles lord it over them, and their high officials exercise

---

60   Adapted largely from "The Virkler Grid" (condensed from *Gifted to Succeed* by Mark and Patti Virkler) and *How to Build a Winning Team* by Mark and Patti Virkler, © 1992, Communion with God Ministries, Cheektowaga, NY, pp. 8–10

authority over them. Not so with you. Instead, whoever wants to become great among you must be your servant'" (Matthew 20:25–26). (Also see Mark 10:42–43 and Luke 22:25–26.)

As a father lovingly serves his family by giving identity, provision and protection, and would die for them, so an apostle serves and sacrifices for his or her organization.

It's for All of Us

It is important to understand that the commission given to the first apostles was also for each of us. As John Eckhardt puts it:

"They were sent into the territories of the earth to convert multitudes of people and incorporate them into the kingdom of God...given (the) power and authority (of the Holy Spirit) to accomplish the task...responsible for teaching, training and instructing the new believers, making them productive citizens of the Kingdom...*Every believer must have this dimension to be a part of fulfilling the Great Commission. This does not make everyone an apostle, but everyone can be apostolic.*"[61]

Remember, in the Old Testament God touched and empowered certain people as he commissioned them for specific tasks. Others relied on the law and the priests to tell them what to do. Not so today. Now, instead of God giving responsibility to selected individuals, He has arranged it so that we can all participate through Christ who lives in us, by the power of the Holy Spirit.

"Wait," you may be saying. "Those are wonderful characteristics, but I don't think they describe me. It looks like apostles are left brain people, and I'm more right brain. I get emotional if things don't go my way. I don't think I could handle

---

61   *Moving in the Apostolic* by John Eckhardt, © 1999, Renew Books, Ventura, CA, pp. 23–24, edited and with italics added.

all that responsibility. Of course, I want the whole organization to succeed, but I'm mostly interested in just doing the best I can in my little area, department or committee."

Read that last sentence again. That's right! Wanting the whole organization to succeed and wanting to do the best you can in your area of responsibility is an apostolic attitude. Congratulations! You are apostolic!

CAN A WOMAN BE APOSTOLIC?

Yes.

NO, REALLY. CAN SHE?

One of the main themes in this book is that the Holy Spirit can empower anyone, regardless of gender or even of primary gifting, to perform in any given role if the need arises. That's why I can say even if you are not an apostle by office or not apostolic in terms of your main gifting, and regardless of gender, when placed in charge of an organization, whatever its size, you are called upon and authorized to be apostolic for the purposes of serving that organization, and God can supernaturally provide for your need to act that way. The Holy Spirit trumps all arguments to the contrary.

Nevertheless, it is reasonable for a woman to be skeptical of this. Or a man, for that matter, if he finds himself under the leadership of a woman occupying an apostolic position. After all, most of the listed attributes and characteristics of apostles seem to fit men better than women, especially those surrounding the idea that an apostle is a "father figure." By contrast, one can much more easily see women in any of the other four roles.

DIFFERENT WIRING

Women. Men. *Vive la différence!* We are wired differently,

and praise God for that. Simplistically put, men are wired to be fathers. Fathers protect, provide, and give identity to their children. These traits do in fact parallel the key apostolic characteristics. On the other hand, women are wired to be mothers. Mothers are nurturing and comforting, and they display discernment, sometimes called intuition. They are also teachers. Those traits more or less encompass pastoring, teaching, the prophetic and even the evangelistic—in other words, the other four five-fold leadership gifts, but not so much the apostolic.

However, there are "smaller wires," if you will, that allow roles to change if necessary. How often have we had a laugh about a man "getting in touch with his feminine side"? Even though a man may be wired to be a father and may exhibit apostolic characteristics, that doesn't mean he cannot be gifted in the five-fold traits that could be more closely associated with women. Obviously, many are, and it is not seen as a challenge to their masculinity.

We don't hear so much about a woman getting in touch with her masculine side, but that's because our culture is double-minded and very touchy about the subject. It doesn't mean she doesn't have one and that it can't be accessed when necessary. Therefore, there is no reason why a woman cannot function in an apostolic role.

If you are a woman placed in an apostolic role and you think your apostolic wires are too small or disconnected, you have only to ask God to re-wire you for the purpose of fulfilling your role. It won't make you any less a woman. For example, let's say you are a single mother. Did you know you can ask God to strengthen you in the areas of protector, provider and identity-giver to the degree necessary to successfully raise your children? You can. Or you can ask someone else to pray this over you.

Depending on your circumstances, you might have to exercise forgiveness toward some of the people you may feel are responsible for putting you in this uncomfortable position, possibly including yourself. You may have to deal with spirits of abandonment or loneliness, or an orphan spirit, but God can take care of those too. If you are a mother whose husband is away, maybe on a tour of military duty, you can pray for a temporary re-wiring. God knows who you are and what you need, and He wants to supply it. I have seen women prayed for in these ways, and it has always been very freeing, comforting, and strengthening.

Keep in mind, too, that nothing prevents you from calling upon members of your extended family—in-laws, siblings, grandparents, etc.—and/or friends to provide needed five-fold input to your situation. In fact, you should be thinking about doing that.

WHAT DOES THE BIBLE SAY ABOUT IT?

The word "apostle" is not found in the Old Testament, although clearly there were apostles we can name, as we saw in Chapter 4. None was a woman, although some women were called to apostolic roles. In Judges 4–5, Deborah is the leader of Israel because none of the men was brave enough to lead. Certainly Esther had an apostolic role when she instructed the Jews to fast for three days and then went before the king to expose Haman's plot against them.

In the New Testament, however, there is a woman identified by Paul as an apostle. She is Junia, mentioned in Romans 16:7.[62] Some say Junia was really a man, but I think not.[63] There are

---

62   "Greet Andronicus and Junia, my relatives who have been in prison with me. They are outstanding among the apostles, and they were in Christ before I was."

63   Some believe her name was really Junias and that translators dropped the "s" by mistake. Others say when it is translated Junias (as in the NIV) the "s" was added to make it a masculine name because the translators couldn't believe it was a woman. However, in Latin the proper masculine name ending is "ius" not "ias." Furthermore, no church commentators before the Middle Ages questioned that Junia was both a woman and an apostle. (From an article on Bible.com: www.bible.com/bibleanswers_result.php?id=141)

many unnamed people who were appointed as apostles along with other elders for the 1ˢᵗ Century churches, and some of them could have been women. Granted, it was probably rare given the Jewish traditions and the culture of the time. In any case, since the evidence indicates there was at least one woman apostle in the New Testament, there is no reason to say a woman cannot hold the office of apostle.

Therefore, why not today? I have no hesitation in saying Heidi Baker is an apostle to the nation of Mozambique and beyond. I believe Mother Teresa was an apostle. There are many others, especially among missionaries.

The way is even clearer if I stick to the question and say there are instances in the Bible of women acting apostolically or donning an apostolic role when called upon to do so. Esther, as I mentioned above, is one example. Another is the woman of Proverbs 31:10–31 who was an apostolic business leader. Whether she was a real woman or an aspirational one, the lesson is that it is good when a woman is apostolic.

So, yes, the answer to the question of whether women can be apostolic is yes.

ACTIVATION EXERCISES

1. Again, without pigeonholing yourself yet, do you see yourself as having many of the characteristics of an apostle? It's perfectly okay if you don't; we're only trying to touch and feel them at this point so that they become more real than just words on a page. Never think an apostle is "better than" and the others are "less or worse than," because that is a lie. All five, and others, are necessary parts of the body (See 1 Corinthians 12:14–31).

2. Try to think of people you know or work with who have these characteristics. Does this discussion help you have a better understanding of those people?

CHAPTER 10

FIVE-FOLD AND THE SAINTS: A GROUP TO ROCK THE WORLD

THE CHARACTERISTICS AND "JOB DESCRIPTIONS" OF EACH AND HOW THEY INTERACT

In this chapter let's expand on each of the five leadership gifts and its role. We'll first review the apostolic role, building on the previous chapter which was devoted to it, and then we'll look at the other four. In the next chapter you will learn how to figure out your particular five-fold gifting, keeping in mind you probably carry more than one such gift.

From our earlier discussions above, and no doubt your own reading and experience, you probably already have a good idea of the roles and characteristics of each of the five-fold ministry gifts of apostle, prophet, evangelist, pastor and teacher. I've gathered and summarized the roles here to make sure we are all on the same page. This will become more important later when we discuss who you are and how you need to relate to others in relationship with you based on who you need to be for them and who they need to be for you, five-fold-wise.

You may or may not be an apostle, a prophet or an evangelist, *per se*, but at any given time you may be called upon or find yourself in a position where you need to function as one of these. For purposes of that season, you *are* an apostle, or a prophet, etc. If you are not comfortable with that appellation, then at least consider yourself apostolic, or prophetic, etc., for purposes of the tasks at hand. In other words, you can exhibit the *characteristics* of an apostle, prophet, etc., for a season, in order to carry out the role of one. This is nothing to be frightened of or timid about, and there is no room here for false modesty. That is just the devil trying to erode your confidence. Resist him and he will flee from you (James 4:7)! Then stand up and be who you are and who you need to be.

As you read the descriptions below, and especially the roles of each of the five leadership gifts, think of them as job descriptions. Obviously, they are not job descriptions such as you would find for specific positions in a business or other organization, but they do describe what is expected of each of the four as he or she shapes and participates on a five-fold leadership team.

APOSTOLIC

ROLE

The apostle's biggest and most important job is to produce other quality leaders who then nurture and strengthen the rest of the people in the organization.

In the marketplace, an apostolic person may be the one in charge of anything from a small committee to a large company as the CEO. He may be a building contractor, an architect, a manager, a coach, a dentist, a band leader, a mayor or a city manager. (Please note that this and corresponding lists

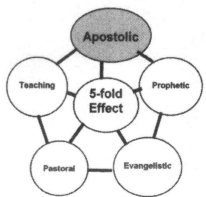

for the other four giftings are not meant to be complete, merely representative.) If young, he may be on a career path to reach one of these positions, possibly starting out as an apprentice, an assistant manager or an administrative assistant.

Different assignments

In the Bible, apostles are given different assignments, both wide and relatively narrow. Peter and Paul are good examples. Although Peter ministered at the house of Cornelius and the Holy Spirit fell upon the Gentiles there (Acts 10), his primary calling was to the Jews. Paul, on the other hand, although he had a heart for the Jews, was primarily called to be an apostle to the Gentiles (Romans 11:13, Galatians 2:8 and 1 Timothy 2:7). He had some pretty bad experiences when he tried to minister to the Jews of his time.

It's the same today. Spheres of apostolic authority may be geographic territories such as nations or cities. They may be people groups, professions, denominations, local churches or church networks, companies, or related to the rest of the seven mountains such as government, education, or arts and entertainment. They may consist of certain types of messages God wants His people to hear, or types of ministries. For example, Dr. Lance Wallnau is foremost among those God has called to promote apostolically the message of seven mountain opportunity.

If you are called to be apostolic, your assigned sphere may be huge, or it may be as small as a two-person committee established for a short-term purpose.

The lesson here is, if after reading the characteristics of an apostle you feel you are such a person, don't go around acting apostolic over everything. Seek God for your assignment.

CHARACTERISTICS[64]

We talked about the apostle's characteristics in Chapter 9 and have touched on them elsewhere. The apostle, or apostolic person, is a servant leader with the heart of a father, a father figure, loving and not domineering. He or she carries great authority but uses it to give identity, provision and protection to the family or organization and to enforce decisions when necessary. He is a vision caster who keeps the organization focused on its mission. Other words to describe an apostle are wise master builder, architect, foundation layer, and atmosphere setter.

Here essentially is a repeat of the list from Chapter 9.

Apostolic people:

- Have a heart passion for the whole of the organization, enterprise or endeavor, and are willing to sacrifice for it
- Are gifted to lead, organize, develop, build and expand; may have administrative ability or at least an appreciation for it
- May have experience in the other five-fold ministries they oversee
- Are less emotional and more structured
- Want to see things organized and running smoothly
- Want all the gifts to be present in a balanced, effective, life giving way
- Judge others by their ability and willingness to fit in
- Influence by helping people to see their value and place in the overall picture
- Get everyone working together as a team; good troubleshooters
- Set others up for success rather than failure

---

64   The Characteristics discussions of each of the five borrow from "The Virkler Grid" (condensed from *Gifted to Succeed* by Mark and Patti Virkler) and *How to Build a Winning Team* by Mark and Patti Virkler, © 1992, Communion with God Ministries, Cheektowaga, NY, pp. 8–10

- Are recognized more for the fruit of what is produced than for a title

I like this description by Paula A. Price:

"Apostles exude authority. Active or dormant, their authority is difficult to disregard. It is the first obvious distinguishing feature. Whatever the situation, the apostle inevitably stands out. He unavoidably finds himself in charge or it is thrust upon him. He competently makes decisions and often casts the deciding vote. Apostles lead when they do not try to; are looked to and relied upon when others seek a strong hand. They command attention and provoke obedience because of God's blatant authority upon them. Extended involvement with an apostle puts you face to face with authority."[65]

PROPHETIC

ROLE

The person with a prophetic gifting has insight and foresight and a good sense of timing to see opportunities and potential pitfalls. He or she analyses situations and advises the apostolic people and others on the leadership team, challenging the status quo, calling attention to problems, encouraging and exhorting. A prophet takes the blueprint the apostolic architect lays out and sees how to make it work, or work better.

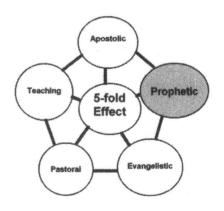

---

65   Paula A. Price, *God's Apostle Revived*, Everlasting Life Publications, Plainfield, NJ, 1994

The prophet's most important job is to train up others who are similarly gifted.

Apostolic people, and sometimes others who are strong willed or who lack self-confidence but try to hide it, often have trouble receiving from a prophetic person. They don't want advice. However, Matthew 10:41 says, "Anyone who receives a prophet because he is a prophet will receive a prophet's reward, and anyone who receives a righteous man because he is a righteous man will receive a righteous man's reward." I'm not sure what a "prophet's reward" is, but if God is promising it then it must be good.[66] Remember this if you have trouble listening to advice from an appropriate source, or if the people you are prophetically serving want to give you a hard time. Work on your understanding of how the five-fold leadership people are supposed to cooperate as a team.

I didn't have this book to help me and had no idea of the five-fold leadership concept when I started a new job as CEO of Kayser-Roth Corporation, a large apparel company. Bo Kenan, the VP of Human Resources, kept coming to me to report things going on in the company and bringing me creative management ideas that I thought were far outside his HR bailiwick. At first, it was annoying. "How does he know all this, and why is he meddling in other people's business? And my business too, for that matter," I would ask myself. It turned out, however, that I really needed to know the things Bo was telling me, and as soon as I got over my petty territorialism and began to respect his abilities both within and outside his official organization chart responsibilities, I realized

---

66   I've heard excellent teaching on this from Bill Johnson, Senior Leader of Bethel Church in Redding, CA, and others. Of course, the emphasis is not on a specific reward itself, but rather the principle that if you accept, respect, and treat well a person who represents God, whether prophet or otherwise, then God will do the same for you. In the case of a prophet, if you respect the word he or she gives you, you will benefit from the realization of that word. Heeding a word that comes from God always brings reward. God knows what you need and is ready to supply it.

he was an invaluable team member. He was providing much needed prophetic insight, identifying opportunities and saving the company from many potential pitfalls. I didn't have to accept all his advice, but I needed to hear it and weigh it as an important part of the decision-making process. I almost missed out on enjoying a good taste of The Five-fold Effect, and I hope this book can help you avoid my mistake.

In the marketplace, a prophetic person might be found as a strategic planner, a financial manager such as a CFO, or a marketing person (who may also be evangelistic). He could be an artist, a writer, a composer, a social reformer, inventor or entrepreneur. Or, like Bo Kenan (who also had pastoral gifting, by the way), he or she could be anyone who has the requisite characteristics and in whom the apostolic person puts trust and calls upon or listens to for prophetic-type input, regardless of place on an organization chart. Likewise, it could be someone outside the company such as a friend, mentor, or life coach.

In *Good to Great*, Dick Cooley, then–CEO of Wells Fargo, comments on hiring outstanding people: "If I'm not smart enough to see the changes that are coming, they will."[67] In five-fold terms, he is saying he values prophetic input.

CHARACTERISTICS

Prophetic people:
- Have insight and foresight
- Are creative and have a heart for creativity and inspiration, and for the Creator
- Have a good sense of timing to see opportunities, marketplace needs (such as consumer demand for new product ideas), and potential pitfalls.
- Are problem solvers and developers, able to improve on others' ideas and plans.

---

67   *Op. cit.*, p. 42.

- Are not so much analytical as intuitive
- Are emotional, experiencing both highs and lows
- Are not afraid to call attention to problems
- Are encouraging while being exhortative

EVANGELISTIC

ROLE

Evangelists get the word out about the good news, whether it is the Good News of the Gospel (which comes from words that mean "good words" or "good tale") or the good news about how wonderful a company's products and services are. Evangelists win friends and customers and thereby create the means for growth. In the marketplace they may be salespeople; marketing, advertising and public relations people; and recruiters. They also evangelize within the organization, helping people to feel good about it, keeping them abreast of the latest news and accomplishments of the

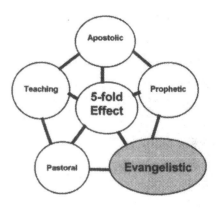

organization and all on the same page regarding its philosophy and goals. They may function alongside trainers and teachers in that role.

The main responsibility of an evangelist is to teach others how to do "evangelism," that is, to do sales and marketing-type tasks or, if sales and marketing is not their job, then to have a sales and marketing attitude. At the very least, that involves fostering a culture where everybody talks favorably about the company to outsiders and each other alike, every chance they get.

CHARACTERISTICS

Evangelistic people:
- Are persuasive
- Are positive
- Are intense and enthusiastic
- Have a heart for winning friends, converts, customers (harvest)
- Want people to see the benefits they see

PASTORAL

ROLE

Like shepherds, pastoral people have and exercise compassion for those struggling to find their place in life, or in the organization. They are interested in people's development and growth. Sometimes they are "hand holders," coming alongside people who need reassurance, especially during times of stress or change, urging them to "keep the faith," so to speak. Or they may deal with those who need to be gently eased out of the organization and given new direction for their lives and careers.  In the marketplace they may be found in roles such as human resources people, coaches, ombudsmen, or outplacement people. They may be counselors, doctors, psychologists, receptionists, waitresses, retail clerks, or workers in other service-type occupations.

CHARACTERISTICS

Pastoral people:

- Are compassionate, loving and protective
- Want to heal hurts and "fix things"
- Have a heart for other people
- Are drawn to people who have needs
- Are sensitive, though sometimes to a fault
- Dislike conflict and confrontation and just want everybody to "get along"
- Willing to sacrifice for the flock, as are apostles, but more susceptible to suffering from "wolf bites"

TEACHING

ROLE

Teacher-type people understand the vision and have the desire and ability to translate it for others into practical action in each functional area. They provide orientation and training for everyone and clearly communicate the organization's goals, philosophies, values and plans to all who need to know. We may find them as trainers, coaches, teachers, and managers. They may be lawyers, technical writers, investigative journalists or researchers.

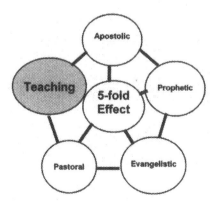

A certain amount of teaching skill is required for most management positions. Often a manager must be able to communicate the "how-to" of his or her subordinates' jobs, operating instructions, orders from higher management, and so on, as well as his own orders with instructions on how to carry them out if necessary. This is consistent with being "apt to teach," one of the 1 Timothy 3:2 qualifications for being a church elder (NIV).[68]

CHARACTERISTICS

Teachers:

- Have a passion for truth and want to share it with others
- Are good communicators or presenters, articulate orally and in writing
- Understand the whys and wherefores of the organization's inside communications needs and can develop good teaching materials and resources
- Are analytical and will research and study their subject before presenting, to make sure they are correct
- Are more structured and less emotional

SUMMARY OF ROLES

Let's further summarize the roles using language based on descriptions from a Regent University study[69] of the so-called "motivational gifts" from Romans 12, which closely parallel the five-fold gifts of Ephesians 4:11–16. (See Chapter 11 for more on this study.)

---

68   I like the Amplified Version's "be a capable and qualified teacher," and later in Titus 1:9, "able...to give stimulating instruction."

69   Dorena Della Vecchio, Ph.D, and Bruce Winston, Ph.D, "A Seven-Scale Instrument to Measure the Romans 12 Motivational Gifts and a Proposition that the Romans 12 Gift Profiles Might Apply to Person-Job Fit Analysis," Working Paper, School of Leadership Studies, Regent University, Virginia Beach, VA, October 2004, p. 2

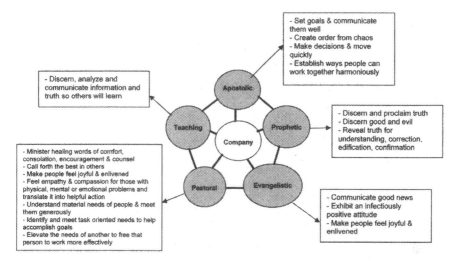

Figure 10–1: Typical Five-Fold Roles in an Organization

WHY DO WE NEED THEM ALL?

It should be fairly obvious that each of the five-fold roles is important and needed. They all work together to create a complete set of required skills and gifts, and they provide important checks and balances for each other.

Don't worry if your organization doesn't have at least five people in it, however. That's not required. As we've said, God usually endows each individual with more than one gift, although usually one or two are predominant. Also, it's likely that each of the five is not needed to the same degree. It depends on the mission of the organization. So if you are heading a committee of two people, don't worry. God has already given you the apostolic gifting to go along with your authority in the situation. He may also have given you a measure of evangelistic fervor as well, for example. Maybe the person you are working with is a good teacher or is very perceptive, i.e., prophetic. If not, maybe you can enlist a friend to give you some insights and counsel if you share your situation with him or her at Starbucks from time to time.[70] Maybe you don't even need a pastoral person this time.

Don't Lose Your Balance

Now, even though I did say you might not need all five of the gifts in equal measure, and occasionally might not need one or two of them at all, the other side of that coin is that you don't want them to be unbalanced. Two apostolic people at the top of an organization can be a recipe for conflict because both will have strong wills and strong ideas about what needs to be done, and these may not agree.[71] There might be a power struggle, even though egos should have been checked at the door. So you should avoid that sort of situation unless you had no choice as to who was assigned to your committee, again using the very small organization as an example, although the principle applies anywhere. If you do have another apostolic person on the team you are in charge of and you recognize the potential pitfall (or are warned of it by a perceptive advisor or member of the team), it's best to have a frank and loving talk with that person to set boundaries or operating ground rules and iron out potential conflict before it occurs.

Beyond that, if you don't have a reasonably balanced five-fold set, depending on your needs and mission, your organization will tend toward one extreme or another, like this (again, drawing from "The Virkler Grid" and translating it to the marketplace):

- The Apostle, left alone, will build a super-organized organization, with not much room for mistakes. All

---

70   I know there are other coffee shops besides Starbucks, but the name has become an icon for a convenient, comfortable gathering place for social interaction among small groups of people.

71   And it may not be a matter of who is right and who is wrong. Either one of two different visions can lead to just as successful an organization, given the wise and intentional employment of five-fold leadership to carry out the one that is chosen.

programs and initiatives will be imposed from on high, and personal initiative will not be appreciated. (Remember Fred from CupKake City.)

- The Prophet will build a legalistic organization because no one is there to challenge his interpretation of what he is saying, and eventually it will become more man-centered than Holy Spirit centered. A company of Pharisees is no fun!
- The Evangelist will go for higher sales and more customers at any cost, ignoring customer service and sound financial stewardship.
- The Pastor will try to keep everybody happy and meet the social needs of each and every employee at the expense of the central mission of the organization. There may be lots of office parties, but not much real work will get done.
- The Teacher will try to interpret the company's rules to the letter and will not let anybody veer from them lest they violate the organization's "theology," if you will. He will allow only one interpretation of right and wrong, i.e., "the truth," and it will be his.

THE PRICE OF OMISSION

Too much emphasis on one or more of the gifts, which we just discussed, is one side of the coin. The other side is not enough emphasis on, or the absence of, one or more that may be critical to the success of your organization or endeavor. Just as nature abhors a vacuum, so apparently does supernature. If one of the important gifts is missing, something much less desirable will be supplied by the enemy. Here is a list of such vacuum-fillers, provided by the well-known prophet Bob Jones.[72]

---

72   Bob Jones, speaking at "The Time is Now" conference, Catch the Fire Raleigh Church, Raleigh, NC, September 30, 2011.

Legalism takes the place of the Apostle.
Opinion takes the place of the Prophet.
Debate takes the place of the Evangelist.
Judgment takes the place of the Pastor.
Criticism takes the place of the Teacher.

Unless you want these unproductive spirits running amok in your organization, take care to have the corresponding five-fold gifts available to you if they are needed.

**Figure 10–2: Don't Clown Around with
Substitutes for the Five-Fold Gifts**

BE OPEN TO MULTIPLE GIFTING

We've already seen that most people have more than one gift. Sometimes they will surprise you, as did Bo Kenan, the VP of Human Resources in the apparel company.

Another type of surprise is when someone you think has one gift suddenly jumps into another one, if only for a season. Bill Caldwell is a good example. As Sales VP and an outstanding salesman, Bill had a key role in putting L'eggs® pantyhose on the map (the ones that came in the plastic eggs). He was a true evangelist for the company. I was the Marketing VP, and Marketing and Sales had a cordial if sometimes tense relationship, mostly because, at least in those days, sales people thought marketing people were out-of-touch ivory tower types (not entirely wrong), and marketing people had a culture of looking down their noses at the folks who had to deal with actual customers. But Bill and I liked each other, and he was well-known for being very good at what he did.

L'eggs Products Company was doing very well. Good products, broad distribution, effective advertising, an excellent reputation with the retailers and consumers, and the leading market share by a wide margin. In other words, an outstanding marketing program, thank you very much.[73]

One day Bill said, "We should run some promotions to round out the advertising campaigns." We had distributed some cents–off coupons in our magazine ads but had never done any promoting beyond that, such as giving allowances to our retailers to offer special price reductions on certain products or for certain time periods, or sponsoring special events to draw attention to the brand, such as a women's 10K race.

"Why?" I said. "We're doing very well without spending money on promotions." I was of the "If it ain't broke, don't fix it" school and quite legalistic. Besides, all sales people want, in typical

---

73   I was not the architect of the L'eggs marketing strategy, however. That distinction belongs to David E. Harrold. Dave began his marketing career at General Mills and in 1968 came to Hanes Corporation in Winston-Salem, NC (later acquired by Sara Lee Corporation), maker of the leading brand of women's hosiery for department stores. There he developed the revolutionary idea of marketing quality women's hosiery through supermarkets and drugstores using a direct-to-store distribution system similar to bread and soft drinks instead of going through wholesalers or retailers' warehouses. In 1969 he hired me as marketing manager to help take L'eggs into test market and eventual national rollout. We ran the secret "V–1" project from windowless offices in the bowels of Hanes' giant Weeks plant for a year before going public, out of concern that Hanes' department store buyers would fear competition from supermarkets and revolt. Fortunately, they didn't.

unbridled evangelistic fashion, is to spend the company's money on frivolous pandering to the retailers who carry our products, right? Weren't the profit margins we were giving them good enough already?

Bill's argument was very simple. "We're doing well, but why not see if we can do even better? Let's at least try it." I couldn't disagree with that. In five-fold terms, here was the top company evangelist sharing with me his prophetic wisdom! Together we developed a plan that we recommended to the president, who approved it. The plan worked, sales and profit soared, and a culture of mutual respect and trust was formed between the Sales and the Marketing departments (and Bill and me) that impacted the culture of the rest of the company from that time onward, surviving several organization changes. Bill saw an opportunity and became who he needed to be for the team at that time. We didn't know it then, but we were enjoying a generous taste of The Five-fold Effect.

"Pastor" as a Misnomer

For the majority of people holding the title "pastor" the title is a misnomer and is a hindrance to an adequate understanding of the five-fold ministry. In both the Hebrew and the Greek the word has to do with shepherding, i.e., the feeding and leading of sheep. Hence, we often hear a congregation referred to as "the flock," who must be "protected" by the "pastor" or shepherd, usually from false doctrine or perceived false doctrine. Although protection is an apostolic role, it is applied here in a much more pastoral sense because of an underlying assumption that members of the flock, like sheep, are incapable of thinking for themselves. Furthermore, this very pastoral way of looking at things denies the fact that the leader of a church body is necessarily *apostolic*, even if he or she happens to have pastoral gifting.

In addition, it fosters the practice of hierarchical control that we so often see in churches where pastors maintain a power position exercising control over the flock. That is not Christian leadership, as we know from Matthew 20:25–26. There is little freedom for the congregants to seek revelation outside the belief systems of their pastors or denominations. They might "make a mistake" or "be deceived," which is code for falling outside the control of the leadership. Certainly we need sound teaching and training, but in the end it should be the Holy Spirit who guides us, not merely our leaders.

Moreover, to the extent this domineering "pastoral" leadership clouds understanding of five-fold ministry, which itself is labeled by many as "not for today" or even heretical, it hurts the pastors themselves. Because five-fold is a reality whether it is recognized or not, a typical pastor is expected to carry the burden of all five. He or she must be apostle, prophet, evangelist, and teacher, as well as pastor in the true sense of the word. The average person may have one or more of these gifts in good measure, and may even be able to operate in all of them for short periods of time, but it takes a huge amount of energy to do so. That is why so many pastors burn out or fall to temptation before they get old enough to enjoy the fruits of their labor. It is also why 59% of the churches in this country have no more than about 100 weekly attendees.[74] That number is actually higher than the number of people a pastor can adequately pastor, if he is truly pastoring, i.e., ministering to the personal and spiritual needs of each person in the congregation

---

74   The median is 75 attendees. 50% of churches are smaller than that, and 50% are larger. The mean, or average, is 186, due to the influence of the relatively few very large churches. 90% of America's churches have 349 or fewer participants and account for 50% of all churchgoers. (National Congregations Study, Duke University, Dr. Mark Chaves, Director, www.soc.duke.edu/natcong/index.html) My guess is that the other 50% of people choose larger churches because they are better "fed" there, whether because of serious five-fold governance or simply because the larger churches can afford to hire multiple "pastors," or both.

on a one-on-one basis, a time-consuming task. Yet that is what is expected.

In churches where five-fold is understood and practiced, "senior leader" is becoming popular as a title. Some even go so far as to use the term "apostle" or "elder" as a title or as an honorific bestowed upon or assumed by the senior leader. The other four leadership roles are shared by other people, whether they are other staff members, "elders," or volunteers. Whatever the leader's title, it should not be a confusing, misleading misnomer.

You're probably not going to run into this situation in a business setting, but if this "misnomering" is going on in your church you may want to consider how to start on the road to correcting it. It will absolutely stand in the way of your church ever being able to practice five-fold leadership and to equip its members to understand and practice it in the marketplace.

ACTIVATION EXERCISES

1. Review this chapter, thinking about the roles and characteristics of each of the five-fold gifts, and see which set of characteristics seems to fit you best. (It may be more than one.)

2. Think about other people you are in close relationship with, or team members in one or more organizations you are in, and do the same for them.

3. Can you recall any instances where you or your organization experienced a little of The Five-fold Effect when one or more of the five-fold gifts came into play and resulted in improved relationships or performance? List them.

CHAPTER 11

Who Are You?

How to Discover Your Five-Fold Gifting (and That of Others)

As suggested in the Activation Exercises in the previous chapter, read the Roles and Characteristics again. See if you think any particular set describes you better than the others. Chances are, your five-fold gifting is in that area. Understand that more than one of the sets may have elements that describe you. That is because, as we've said before, God rarely limits our gifts to only one. The apostle Paul was also a teacher and an evangelist. You, too, probably have some gifting in more than one of the five areas. However, one of them should stand out as seeming stronger than the others.

After arriving at some idea of what your five-fold gifting is, ask two or three trusted friends, including your spouse if you are married, which set they think best describes you. They may not agree with you or each other completely, but it is likely there will be general agreement.

Take a Test

You don't really need to take a behavioral or psychological test to get a pretty good idea who you are in five-fold terms. However, those can be fun and can also be revealing and thought-provoking. Here is one that is easy to do. In his book, *Gifted to Succeed*, Dr. Mark Virkler calls the five-fold gifts "heart motivations." He offers a Heart Motivation Profile with 45 questions, as well as other exercises, to help you discover your giftedness.[75] You can complete the Profile for yourself and then ask three friends to complete an "Observation Assessment" of you for comparison. When these are combined with the results of a "Life Experience Profile," you will have a clear picture of your Heart Motivations, corresponding to five-fold gifts. I recommend you get Mark's book and go through it carefully, doing all the exercises if you really want to get a good assessment of your gifting and how to apply it to your ministry.

Another easy test, in spite of its long academic-sounding title, is "A Seven-Scale Instrument to Measure the Romans 12 Motivational Gifts and a Proposition that the Romans 12 Gift Profiles Might Apply to Person-Job Fit Analysis" offered by Regent University and which I first mentioned in Chapter 10. To take the test online, go to www.gifttest.org. It's free. There is also an interesting academic paper available that gives the background and explanation of how the test was developed.[76]

---

75   *Gifted to Succeed* by Mark and Patti Virkler, pp. 29–43. Order online at www.cwgministries.org

76   Go to this Web page if you want to read the academic working paper: www.regent.edu/acad/global/publications/working/DellaVecchio-Winston%20Romans%2012%20gift%20test%20and%20profiles%20manuscriptdv.pdf. Or, since you can't just click on a link in this book and that's an awful lot to type into your browser without making a mistake, go to the Regent University Website, www.regent.edu, and enter "motivational gifts" in the Search field at the top of the home page. A link to the study should come up.

Five-Fold versus the Romans 12 "Motivational Gifts"

The Regent University paper distinguishes between the five-fold ministry gifts of Ephesians 4 and the so-called motivational gifts of Romans 12. It quotes Jack Hayford who warns, "distinguishing among the gifts of Romans 12:6–8 (from the Father), the gifts of 1 Corinthians 12:8–10 (from the Holy Spirit), and those in Ephesians 4, which are explicitly given by Christ the Son, are pivotal in comprehending the whole scope of spiritual Gifts."[77]

Not everyone agrees on the importance of this distinction, but to me the important thing is that all these gifts are from God. I agree the Romans 12 gifts are not offices, they have a fundamentally different purpose from those in Ephesians 4, and they are not interchangeable, but their characteristics are close enough to those of the five-fold gifts as to be comparable for our purposes here. They are comparable in the sense that they can be thought of as "indicators of life purpose, thus there may be applications of motivational gifts to the study of job satisfaction and performance in organizations."[78] And, of course, that's exactly what we're talking about in this book, but more proactively. We're not only trying to prevent forcing square pegs into round holes. We're also willing to reshape some of the holes, and some of the pegs, so that the pegs and holes shape up to a desirable whole (a holy whole?).

A minor problem is that there are seven motivational gifts and only five of the others. Based on the definitions available, I would stack them up against each other this way:

---

77   Hayford, J., Ephesians. In J. W. Hayford, J. Horner and S. Middlebrook (Eds.), *Spirit Filled Life Bible* (1991), Nashville, TN, Thomas Nelson Publishers, p. 1792, paraphrased.

78   *Op. cit.*, p. 2

Table 11-1: Comparison of Five-Fold and Romans 12 Gift Characteristics

Romans 12 Gift	Regent Study Definition	Corresponding Five-Fold Gift
1. Ruling	- Set goals & communicate them well - Create order from chaos - Make decisions & move quickly - Establish ways people can work together harmoniously	Apostolic
2. Perceiving	- Discern and proclaim truth - Discern good and evil - Reveal truth for understanding, correction, edification	Prophetic
3. Encouraging	- Minister healing words of comfort, consolation, encouragement & counsel - Call forth the best in others - Make people feel joyful & enlivened	Pastoral Evangelistic
4. Mercy	- Feel empathy & compassion for those with physical, mental or emotional problems and translate it into helpful action	Pastoral
5. Giving	- Understand material needs of people & meet them generously - Manage income, time, energy & skills to exceed normal standards for giving	Pastoral
6. Serving	- Identify and meet task oriented needs to help accomplish goals - Elevate the needs of another (w/o concern for recognition) to free that person to work more effectively	Pastoral (and Administrative)
7. Teaching	- Discern, analyze and communicate information and truth so others will learn	Teaching

So, for example, if you score high on "Ruling" in the Regent test,[79] chances are you have many apostolic characteristics. If you score high on "Mercy," you might be pastoral.

If you decide to use either or both the Virkler and the Regent University gift tests, you should be able to triangulate and discover who you are without much trouble.

TEST AGAIN IN A FEW YEARS

I have found it's a good idea to take these tests again after a few years. People change as they learn and mature both in the natural and spiritually, and it is interesting and helpful to see the development. Also, if you are on or leading the same team for several years, or different teams made up of many of the same people, you can avoid pigeonholing yourself or anyone else on the team by recognizing that passions, calling and/or skill sets may have changed. I recently completed both of these tests or profiles

---

79   *Ibid.*, pp. 3–4. Also see Figure 10–1 in Chapter 10.

again myself after an interval of several years. There were some shifts.

OTHER PERSONALITY TESTS

There are many other personality, behavioral or psychological tests available that can be useful in gaining an understanding of why people act the way they do, to predict success in various fields of work or study, to aid in placing people in the right jobs, and to help groups of co-workers to better understand each other. One of the earliest is the well-known Rorschach inkblot test introduced in 1921. Many people remember, and may have taken, the Myers-Briggs Type Indicator test which was developed during World War II. A currently very popular test is the DiSC assessment, which identifies four personality types: Dominance, Influence, Steadiness and Conscientiousness. It is used widely in Fortune 500 companies and in other for-profit and non-profit organizations.[80]

In his book, *Discover Your Spiritual Gifts*, Dr. C. Peter Wagner points out that there are in fact 25 spiritual gifts listed or mentioned in the Bible, and he identifies three more that are not specifically mentioned, for a total of 28. (Remember our earlier discussion about lists in the Bible not necessarily being exhaustive.) He discusses how you can determine what yours are and includes a simple questionnaire to help you do this. I found the book engaging and very useful, and I enjoyed taking the test.[81]

Stay Focused on Five-Fold

I think it is good to use one or more of these tests in an

---

80   See http://en.wikipedia.org/wiki/DISC_assessment. The test is based on the research of William Moulton Marston and later work by John Grier. There are many purveyors of this test who can be found by Googling "DiSC" or "DISC." Dr. Lance Wallnau, for example, has used it extensively in his consulting work for corporations (http://lancelearning.com).

81   *Discover Your Spiritual Gifts, Updated and Expanded* by C. Peter Wagner, Regal Books, Ventura, CA, 2005. Includes the "Wagner-Modified Houts Questionnaire," beginning on p. 87.

organization, especially if it is larger than a handful of people, because they are usually pretty reliable and can be quite helpful, especially in career placement and in predicting how a person might fit into the already established culture of the organization. In many of them you will find parallels with five-fold gifts or heart motivations. However, I do not recommend them as a substitute for determining five-fold gifting. Instead, after using five-fold as the foundation because it is God-given, carries supernatural power, and is the basis for the talents and aptitudes identified in them, these other tests can then help flesh out practical details.

GIFTING DOES NOT EQUAL CALLING

Keep in mind that gifting isn't the same thing as calling. Being gifted with teaching aptitude does not necessarily mean you are called to be a teacher, *per se*, any more than prophetic gifting necessarily means your destiny is to be a prophet. However, gifting is good preparation for calling and may be indicative if not definitive.

Performing the exercises below with your co-workers is something I recommend you do when you find yourself in an apostolic role, even if your strongest gift is not apostolic.

ACTIVATION EXERCISES

1. Complete the Regent University motivational gifts test and the Virkler Heart Motivation Profile. Are you surprised by the results or do they confirm what you've already thought about yourself? If surprised, think about why that is so and what you might need to do to resolve the discrepancy between what you thought and what the profiles indicate.

2. Do the results give you more confidence in your calling or interests and in your desire and ability to live them out?

3. Now that you have a good idea who you are in the five-fold scheme of things, go back to Chapter 10 and review your particular "job descriptions."

CHAPTER 12

APPLICATION HANDBOOK, PART 1 – GETTING STARTED

"Brothers, what shall we do?" (Acts 2:37b)

Are you ready to try this yourself? Let's say there is an organization you know of that's ripe for the application of the five-fold paradigm of leadership and organizational transformation. Why, that would be all organizations, wouldn't it? In that case, then, you do know of one and we're off to a good start. The question is, "How do I apply all this?" Here and in the next three chapters we will look at practical application of all the theory we've been talking about.

What You Can Do Where You Are

Remember, the concepts work equally well for any size organization or unit, whether it's a business, an athletic team and its coaching staff, a club, the police department, a government unit, or a committee, and so on—wherever people are gathered to perform tasks together.

The first question to ask is, "What is my five-fold role in the situation at hand?" It will be different for different relationships you have. Just as a man is simultaneously a father, husband, son, brother, uncle, nephew, etc., your co-workers may look to you for your leadership and appreciate the way you try to protect them (apostolic/pastoral) while your boss may rely on your ability to translate company goals into action (teaching/evangelistic). Of course, this could change. Organizations, like life, are not static. They develop. Your roles will change from time to time, and you will need to be sensitive to this as seasons and circumstances change. But for now . . .

GET AN ATTITUDE — YOU ARE PRESIDENT OF YOUR JOB

Seeking the Holy Spirit for wisdom and guidance, think of yourself as president of your job—the *apostle* over your area of responsibility, however large or small, even if your role on the five-fold team is not the apostolic one. It is a very freeing thought that can fill you with the courage and boldness to act like a leader and not a follower.[82] Look for ways of doing your job better and better and of adding as much value as you can to the enterprise. Just don't forget you are a servant leader, serving those who work with or under you just as much as those above you in the organization structure.

Next, consider these guidelines on what to do if you find yourself in an apostolic role. After this, we'll look at what to do if you are in one or more of the other four roles.

---

82 Note, there is nothing wrong with or inferior about being a follower. However, if you are in charge of something, or responsible for something, such as your job, however narrowly drawn, you are the leader for whatever that may be. It is important to know how to act like one.

Your Apostolic Role

Okay, so let's say you find yourself in a situation where you have the apostolic role. Maybe you are a company president. Since there are relatively few of those, let's say maybe you are a division or department head. Maybe you are a committee chairman. Or maybe you simply have a job or a task to be performed that involves one or more other people and you are in charge or feel the need and call to take charge. That makes you apostolic for that situation. Now, let's flesh out your job description a little more. Here's what to do.

You have determined who you need to be for your co-workers, in this case to be their leader, their "apostle." Now you must determine who your co-workers need to be for you, and for the enterprise. This is where you look around and say, "Who are my prophetic or visionary people?" and, "Who are my evangelistic people?" and so on. "How can I get them to understand their five-fold role and work together and with me as a leadership team to help me see and then communicate the vision and equip the other employees or committee members to do their best work for the good of the enterprise?"

Again, a key is to be *intentional* about people's selection and placement to be sure it is consistent with their gifting and calling and to create an environment where they work in concert toward a common vision. Ideally, you get to select your team, but in the more likely event that someone else has already selected them, you must work with what you have unless you can manage to get anyone dis-assigned or bring anyone else on board. However, you can also use gifted people outside the immediate organization for consultative input.

Discerning Purpose, Calling and Destiny

Here's an important reminder. One of your responsibilities

is to help discern God's purpose and calling for everyone in the organization and to help them position themselves to walk in it. Not only will this help them to thrive and find their destiny, but also it will enhance The Five-fold Effect as the organization experiences greater unity of purpose and greater effectiveness among the various people whose work contributes to its success. There is also an important element here of helping people rise to a higher functioning level, e.g., equipping them well enough to qualify for promotion. This benefits not only them but the overall enterprise too.

Of course, you are not expected to do this personally for everyone in the organization if it consists of more than a handful of people, but you are responsible to see that it is done and to monitor it. (See Chapter 14 for a more thorough discussion of this.)

First Step: Daily Prayer Responsibility

As the apostolic leader in the situation, you have a particular responsibility to hear from God and to pray for the enterprise and your co-workers.

Just as the five-fold gifting in Ephesians 4 applies to any organization, I believe 2 Chronicles 7:14 applies not just to nations, but also to all the endeavors of believers. You know this familiar passage:

"If my people, who are called by my name, will humble themselves and pray and seek my face and turn from their wicked ways, then will I hear from heaven and will forgive their sin and will heal their land."

If you are a believer then you are among "the people who are called by my name." "Heal their (your) land" means healing for whatever you are praying about. In this case "land" is the organization or enterprise over which you have been given charge. It is about taking dominion over your sphere of responsibility and influence for the Kingdom. Often, too, it is about taking back territory stolen by the enemy.

Feel free to pray in any way God may lead you. For a start, you can consider a prayer crafted from 2 Chronicles 7:14 and Ephesians 4:11–16 which I have included at the end of this chapter and in Appendix B.

A CONDITIONAL PROMISE

Allow me to preach for a moment. Often we focus on the wonderful promise from God in this passage from 2 Chronicles without considering the conditions He requires for it. The hard part always seems to be "humbling" yourself and turning from your wicked ways. Most of us don't think of ourselves as having wicked ways. I may sin, yes, but "wicked ways"? I don't think so. Well, let's think again. It is, in fact, about sin, and if that's not wicked I don't know what is. Ask the Holy Spirit each day to show you if you have any sin that needs to be dealt with. There is no condemnation in this, as there would have been under the Law (Romans 8:1). Today, when the Holy Spirit reminds you of sin it is because He wants to help you deal with it. He is about to heal you of it if you will let Him. Although we often use the word "conviction" when referring to the Holy Spirit's reminders, it is not about judge and jury convicting you of a crime. Rather, it means you are now "convinced" you have a sin and are ready to confess it so you can be forgiven and move on toward the healing of it.[83]

First and foremost, to "humble" yourself means to acknowledge the lordship of God. After that it means to "repent," another word unnecessarily charged with guilt. We don't do sack cloth and ashes today. It just means "feel regret over a sin (or a wicked way!), and

---

83   We may refer to someone as "a man of strong convictions," usually a positive assessment describing the virtue of single-mindedness. He is convinced of certain things and won't be moved. He is probably not a convicted criminal now serving 12 years for armed robbery.

change the way you think about what you are doing." That's not so hard to do, although it may take practice in the case of deep rooted sin because that requires the breaking of strong habits.

The point here is that you want to remove any sin that is hindering you from doing a good job, or that is hindering the Holy Spirit from working through you to do it.

If you haven't already done so, right now flip to the end of this chapter (or Appendix B) and read the crafted prayer there. Daily, say a prayer like this or one of your own choosing.

ESTABLISH INTERCESSORY PRAYER

Intercessory prayer is very important as well. I recommend you enlist others to pray for you and your work and for your co-workers. Keep the intercessors informed periodically of progress to be thanking God for and of issues for prayer direction.

Next Steps

Next, review the five-fold characteristics and roles from Chapter 10. Then assess and satisfy the needs of your situation in five-fold terms.

1. Assess Your Needs. Ask, "Would the task or enterprise need or benefit from prophetic (perceptive, intuitive, discerning) input, evangelistic skill (getting the word out, generating favorable opinion for the project), pastoral skill (helping people get through a new or challenging situation), and/or teaching skill (explaining the vision to others in the group, training)?" Depending on the situation, especially if it is a very small organization, you may or may not need all five, but you probably need at least three. If there are more than four or five people involved, you probably do need all five gifts, even if one or more must be sought from outside the immediate group. Review the "job descriptions" or roles of the five-fold gifts in Chapter 10 to refresh your memory.

2. Make a list of the five-fold gifts that are needed. Add other gifts and skills you may need, such as administration.

3. Match the list with the people involved. As best you can, again with the help of the Holy Spirit and the discussion of characteristics in Chapter 10, try to list who has which characteristics. Who is your prophetic person (or persons), etc.? Who is administrative, if that's a needed skill? And so on. Keep in mind that you yourself may have one or more of the needed gifts. Discuss the roles and characteristics with the team that is forming, to see if there is agreement as to who has what gifts or heart motivations. Complete the Virkler and/or Regent University tests, described in Chapter 11, on everyone involved.

4. This would also be a good time to prophesy over each person, asking the Holy Spirit to reveal to you where each one might fit best on the team or in the organization based on an alignment of the organization's needs with the gifts, calling and destiny of each person. Depending on circumstances, it may or may not be necessary or appropriate to do this out loud, or even with the person present. Just ask the Holy Spirit to speak to you. (Again, see Chapter 14 for more about this.)

   If all of the needed gift bases are covered, whether it is three, let's say, or all five plus some supplemental ones, fine. If not,

5. Fill in the Gaps. Take steps, if possible, to get the missing one(s) into your organization or identify the corresponding resource(s) outside it. If you have the authority or the influence, see if you can change the personnel on your team until you have the kinds of people you need, i.e., "the right people on the bus." If not, then try to get the people who are "on the bus" to sit where they will do the most good

while you help them to become the right people at least for that season.

Meanwhile, see if there is someone outside the team on whom you can rely for needed input. Often this will be a prophetic (or perceptive) person familiar with your situation who can offer input based on your keeping him or her up to date on developments. Possibly it could be a pastoral person from another department whom you could ask to speak to one or more of your people who might be experiencing difficulty. Or you may even want pastoral help for yourself from time to time! Pray and ask God to help you with this too.

Time and time again in ministry situations I have observed the Holy Spirit acting as a Divine usher, directing people who want prayer to exactly the right person He has prepared to pray for them. In the same way, He can bring you the people you need.

6. Teach the Team about Five-Fold. Once the team is in place, find an opportunity to tell them about the five-fold ministry/leadership concept and how you are intending to employ it. Tell them your vision for the enterprise and explain how you see each of them, and yourself, contributing from their five-fold and other skills and talents. Invite them to comment and make suggestions (Do this periodically, not just once.). Ask them how they see themselves as members of the team. With that input, you will probably revise the vision. When that happens, then have a follow up vision casting session. The team will function much more effectively when everyone understands his or her role, your expectations (not to be confused with control), and that their input has been considered.

Your objective, beyond the practical aspects of getting everyone on the same page, is to provide a climate where all the team members have the same spirit, the same mind by revelation, and the belief that they are supposed to be there. This is sometimes called "buy in," and there should be joy in it.

7. Get to Know Your Team. Like most endeavors, business is built on relationships. Mutual knowing, caring, and appreciating helps people to want to work together. This is a process, not just a step (as are several of the other "steps" presented here). As you share the vision, and each team member shares in it, trust is built, ownership is taken on, and everyone feels pride in a job well done. As importantly, the authority you initially have because of your position as leader will be transformed into authority that is given by your team members as they learn to trust you. That is a much stronger kind of authority.

8. Be Prepared to Fulfill a Needed Role Yourself. If you cannot cover the five-fold and other bases needed either within the immediate group or from outside it, maybe because your superiors simply won't allow you to do so, then you may have to "suck it up" and perform the needed role yourself in addition to your apostolic role. Or select one of the other team members and ask her to do it, coaching and equipping her as best you can. Don't worry; it's not forever, only for a season. Ask the Holy Spirit for help.

9. Identify and Form Your Leadership Team. If you are in charge of a large group, these guidelines still apply, but instead of finding a role for everyone, you need to think in terms of a leadership team, the handful of trusted people you will surround yourself with. It doesn't necessarily matter where each of them is located on the organization chart, although most often the five-fold will, or should, correspond to functional titles in the organization. It is obviously best if you can have all five gifts on the immediate team, but if not, it's okay to seek the missing benefits from people who may not be. It is also okay, and

probably necessary if it is a large organization, to have more than five people on the leadership team (but probably no more than about seven because more would stretch what is commonly known as the "effective span of control," although I prefer "span of care."). Also, you probably want to have more than one person in each of the five-fold roles anyway if the organization and task is large and complex enough.

For example, it doesn't hurt to get prophetic input from more than one person. At Grace Church, much of Rodney Odom's five-fold input comes from people not in the official leadership organization chart. That includes not only The 411 Group, but also members of the office staff and trusted spiritual advisors outside the church.

I recall hearing about well-known CEOs receiving insightful input from unlikely sources in their organizations. The popular TV show, "Undercover Boss," provided weekly examples of this. And I get a real kick out of it when Dilbert occasionally seeks prophetic wisdom from his garbage man. Whatever works, but do it with consistency and intentionality.

However, you do not need to, nor should you, act on every piece of input you get. Some of it will be wrong or just plain bad. Even the most gifted and experienced prophet can make mistakes because, as we know from 1 Corinthians 13:9, "For we know in part and we prophesy in part." That's the beauty of having a team and the Holy Spirit so that inputs can be carefully and prayerfully compared and weighed before vision is set, decisions are made, and actions are taken. (Read more about the decision making process in the next chapter.)

If you didn't do it in Step 3, consider administering the Virkler and/or Regent University tests for each person to help them determine their giftedness.

10. <u>Pray every day and over every big decision.</u> Again, see the crafted apostolic prayer at the end of this chapter (and in Appendix B) which you can use as a guide.

11. <u>Maintenance.</u> Your team itself can be considered an "accountability group." Use it as such to periodically assess whether and how you are applying the five-fold principles. Simply establishing five-fold leadership is not enough. It needs maintenance. It must be refreshed from time to time in order for the team to adapt to changing times and circumstances and to avoid being taken for granted. Roles may need to change as people and situations change. New people may join the organization, and others may transfer out or quit. Constant Holy Spirit led refreshment will be needed. (More about the "accountability group" in the next chapter)

12. <u>Intercession.</u> As I said above, intercessory prayer for your work and your co-workers is very important. In a secular environment, you may be the only intercessor. Enlist people you trust to pray, whether they are inside or outside the organization. Keep them informed of your status, including progress and victories to thank God for and issues or problems and opportunities for prayer direction.

Summarizing the Steps – Here are the steps we've just laid out.
First Step: Daily prayer responsibility
Next Steps:
1. Assess your needs.
2. Make a list of the needed five-fold gifts or ministries.
3. Match the list with the people involved.
4. Prophesy over each person.
5. Fill in the gaps, from within or outside the organization.

6. Teach the team about five-fold, and begin the vision casting process.

7. Get to know your team.

8. Be prepared to fill a needed role yourself.

9. Identify and form your leadership team (if a larger organization).

10. Pray every day and over every big decision.

11. Maintenance – use the team as an accountability group.

12. Have intercessors praying.

Keep in mind, this is a process. It is not a recipe or a set of steps that must be rigidly adhered to or the soufflé will be ruined. It is reiterative, and you should constantly review and sometimes retrace or repeat steps as the team develops and matures and the situation changes.

Questions that May Arise

A. "But I'm not in a Christian organization. Can I still use these principles?"

If you are the owner of the company you can certainly choose to openly run it as a Christian company. If you are not, then you must carefully consider your options for how to proceed. First, understand that the principles work whether they are labeled as biblical or Christian or not. Second, consider what works and doesn't work from an evangelistic viewpoint. Usurping the authority you are under (which, remember, is God given even if it is not recognized as such by those who hold it) or rubbing peoples' noses in the fact that you are a Christian or the idea that biblical ways of doing things are the best, will not win friends and influence people in your, or God's, favor. Don't do that. Also keep in mind that there are laws and legal precedents designed to protect others from what they may perceive as unwanted proselytizing.

You must assess the environment you are in and use wisdom on how to proceed. You shouldn't need permission to speak openly about your faith, but you may need permission to talk in terms of five-fold leadership when dealing with your team. The permission, or sanction, can come from your superiors, but even then you have no license to impose it on your team even if you are their boss. Try to explain it to them and see if they are receptive. If you feel they will accept the idea that the apostolic, prophetic and other spiritual gifts are for today or at least have modern-day parallels, then use language such as the Motivational Gifts terms discussed in Chapter 11 or plain old secular language, e.g., "perceiving" instead of "prophetic," "salesman" instead of "evangelist." Avoid speaking in "Christianese."

As a last resort, if you feel you cannot openly discuss with anyone what you want to do regarding five-fold leadership, then go "under cover." Go through the steps above on your own, identifying the people who have the gifts you need for the task at hand. Be who they need you to be for them, and "use" them in the ways they need to be for you and the organization, even if you never say a word to them about what you are doing. You will still experience The Five-fold Effect to some degree. Eventually, you may find you can broach the subject to some or all of your people. At that point, things may begin to take off!

B. "I've been getting the kind of input that you describe from team members for years, and now it seems to me all you are doing is calling it 'five-fold' instead of whatever everybody else calls it. What's with that?"

It's very good that you have been doing this. But I wonder whether you have been doing it systematically and comprehensively and with the kind of intentionality that comes from understanding the biblical basis for it, the whole foundational plan of Ephesians 4:11–16, the inseparability of church and marketplace from God's point of view, and the realization that you can tap into supernatural power with it. If so, you have arrived. If not, then I would say that starting now to use the "five-fold" terminology will serve as a practical reminder of how to think in this paradigm. Whatever the case, keep it up!

C. What if I have two or more prophetic people on my team and they give me conflicting input?

You are fortunate indeed! Before you toss that off as flippancy, let me answer this excellent question on three levels.

First, the input may in fact not be conflicting although it may appear so. Each person providing input may not be seeing the whole picture. 1 Corinthians 13:9 says, "For we know in part and we prophesy in part." You could be hearing different parts of the same truth, like the famous tale of the blind men coming up with different descriptions of an elephant based on which part each one touched.

When my wife, Carol, and I were house hunting in a new city where we were relocating, she prayed and felt God was showing her a Williamsburg Colonial style house. But a friend of hers said, "I think God is showing me a house for you that has long, narrow windows that are two stories tall, and between them is stonework, like maybe a fireplace chimney." A third friend said, "Your house will have silver and gold going up an incline like maybe a staircase." These ideas did not seem compatible, and Carol was confused. Praying again, she felt God answer, "Don't be led by prophecy, but my My Spirit." Instead of looking for a house with these characteristics, we looked for one we liked that met our needs and our budget. When we found it and had peace about it, she asked God to confirm if that was the one, and then we bought it.

Later we realized Carol and her two friends had all seen different views of this same house. It looked Williamsburg Colonial from the street. Inside was an atrium-like family room with tall, narrow windows flanking a two-story stone fireplace chimney. From inside the family room, at the bottom of an exposed staircase leading up to bedrooms, could be seen a guest bathroom with silver and gold wallpaper. Here was further confirmation that God knew which house He had for us! The experience increased our faith that we could trust God to meet our needs.

Second, consider the positions of the people giving the input. Your Finance Director's input in many cases may have more do with his or her area of responsibility than with the whole enterprise. The same may be true for any of the others. Try first to understand what they are talking about and how it might apply narrowly before considering its more general implications.

Third, don't be directed by prophecy, but by the Holy Spirit. As Carol learned when we were looking for the house, we could have wasted a lot of time looking and finding houses that each had one of the characteristics described and then wasted more time anxiously trying to figure out which one God meant, fearing we might miss it. Instead, when we found the one we thought might be for us, it was confirmed by prayer and only later by referring to the prophetic input Carol had received. So don't necessarily take prophetic input literally, whether it is from one person or several, without weighing it, comparing it, discussing it, seeing how it lines up with other situational factors, and asking God to show you what it might mean.

THE PROPHETIC, EVANGELISTIC, PASTORAL, AND/OR TEACHING ROLES

In Chapter 11, you learned some ways to determine what your five-fold gifting is. Now the question comes back around to this: If you are not in the apostolic role, then who do you need to be for the team, for your co-workers? The question applies equally whether you are on an apostolic person's leadership team or not. If you are working with other people on anything, then you are on some kind of team.

If you are on a team of Christians led by an apostolic person who is applying the five-fold principles with intentionality, and if your role is clear and is consistent with your gifting, you are in an ideal situation. Thank God every day for it. (Well, thank God every day for whatever situation anyway, even if not ideal.) Whether you are on such a team or not, your responsibilities are the same. Here are some instructions to follow after again reviewing the five-fold "job descriptions" in Chapter 10:

1. <u>Determine what the five-fold needs of the team are</u>, asking God for wisdom and guidance. Does the leader (and other team members as well) need prophetic input? Why? What would be the nature of such input? For example, is there difficulty in determining the proper direction of the team, i.e., what is our mission; what are our goals? Are there political issues we need to be aware of and navigate through?

   Are we likely to hit rocky spots because we are going to try to do things a new and different way or because we are paving new paths for the enterprise in terms of new products, services or procedures? Then maybe we will need someone with pastoral gifts to hold peoples' hands as we steer the canoe through the rapids.

   Are we going to have to persuade others, including our superiors as well as people in other parts of the company, or outside it, that what we are doing or proposing is good for the business? Then we'll need evangelistic leadership. (All this is similar to the discussion of Question 1 under "Your Apostolic Role," above. Review that now.)

2. <u>Go through this thought process carefully for all the tasks and needs of the team.</u> Try to identify where you can make

the best contribution five-fold-wise, even if it means you have to step outside your official job description. Don't forget, you may have more than one gift to offer.

3. <u>Assess the other team members the same way.</u> Again, this would also be a good time to prophesy over each person, asking the Holy Spirit to reveal where each might fit best based on an alignment of their gifting, calling and destiny with the organization's needs. You don't necessarily have to do this aloud or in the person's presence.

4. <u>Share your thoughts with your leader.</u> If the leader has openly expressed the intention to operate on a five-fold basis, discuss this intention with him or her. The leader is probably seeking this kind of discussion anyway. If not, discuss it to the degree you feel comfortable. If you feel the enterprise would better benefit by having you in a role other than the one you've been assigned, suggest a change. But do not pout if the change is not made. Again, these things are only for a season.

5. <u>Witness by example.</u> Even if the team is not being run according to five-fold ministry principles, you can still make a difference by carrying out your part as if it were. Even if you are not in the apostolic role for the team, <u>you are still president of your job!</u> You are a witness to others and you change the atmosphere because of the Holy Spirit who is within you. It's entirely possible others will see something intriguing in your behavior and ask you about it. That could lead to conversations that might open a door to seeing five-fold ministry in full operation where you are. Also, it could be an opportunity for evangelism, or at least the planting of seeds.

6. <u>Pray every day for the team and over every big decision.</u> Feel free to use the apostolic prayer suggested at the end

of this chapter (also reprinted in Appendix B), based on 2 Chronicles 7:14 and Ephesians 4:11–16.

Summarizing:

1. Determine what the five-fold needs of the team are.

2. Go through this thought process carefully for all the tasks and needs of the team to see where you can best contribute.

3. Assess the other team members the same way.

4. Share your thoughts with your leader.

5. Witness by example.

6. Pray every day for the team and over every big decision.

OTHER QUESTIONS THAT MAY OCCUR TO YOU

1. "What if I'm apostolically gifted but I'm not in charge?" We've said that two apostolic people on the same team can be a recipe for conflict. If you are an employee of a company, there may be no choice for you in the matter. My suggestion is that you and the leader talk about this issue, again using non-church terms if your leader is not someone who embraces the five-fold ministry idea. Agree on ground rules and boundaries, mainly for yourself. Also, because God usually calls apostles to have responsibility for particular spheres as we saw in Chapter 10, it's possible your leader could give you apostolic responsibility for some part of the work at hand, a subdivision of the team perhaps. But make sure it is real, not just made up to avoid a tense situation.

   Your leader is still your leader. He or she was put in that position, and you weren't. She may be senior to you not only in position in the organization, but also in the development of the gifts you have in common. In that case, change your agenda. Learn what you can while you are in the situation. See it for the opportunity that it is, not as a problem. In any case, don't chafe over it. It's only for a season.

2. <u>"What if I'm apostolic and not in charge and the person in charge is not apostolic?"</u> I strongly advise you not to stage a coup! You know the proper question: "Who do I need to be for that person?" Pray that the Holy Spirit will give the leader the apostolic characteristics, or "wiring," needed for the task and the season. God put that person in the place of authority and can certainly back him or her up. Maybe He put you there to help. Look for ways to lend apostolic support to the extent the leader is willing to accept your suggestions and help (This applies in Question 1 as well.). If five-fold is being employed intentionally in the situation, the leader will understand and welcome your help. If it is not, then you must look for ways to approach the situation that are not threatening to him or her. In the meantime, don't neglect the role you've been assigned. If you are supposed to be the evangelistic one, for example, do that too. In everything, build up the leader and the organization.

<u>Impartation of Spiritual Gifts</u>

This is a good place to broach the subject of impartation. One of the ways you can help your team leader is by praying that the Holy Spirit will impart through you a measure of your apostolic gift to him or her. Ideally, you need the person's permission to do this so that he can receive the impartation when it is given. The prayer might go something like this: "Lord, thank you for the gifts you have given me, particularly the gift of apostolic leadership. I pray now that you would impart this gift to (Name)." Then, addressing the person, "(Name), as God has gifted me with apostolic characteristics, in Jesus' name I impart these to you by the power of the Holy Spirit. Freely I have received, now freely I give.[84] Receive this impartation now, in the name of Jesus."

A prayer of impartation is appropriate for any of the five-fold gifts, and other gifts as well, and may be employed if you find gaps in your five-fold team that cannot be filled by people already possessing the gifts in question. However, don't think of impartation as a spiritual magic pill that instantly endows people with mature ability in some area. More often, it may be the planting of a seed that then needs nurturing to grow and mature.

See Appendix C for a more thorough discussion of impartation of spiritual gifts.

3. <u>"What if the person in charge is not apostolic and neither am I?"</u> First of all, are you *sure* the person is incapable of acting apostolically in the situation? Don't make an assumption based on a personality or gifting profile that God will not show him what to do or that he cannot learn. Pray for him as you would for every other member of the team. Depending on your own five-fold role and your relationship with this leader, you might make suggestions about how he can seek advice from apostolic people who may or may not be on the team. You may be able to find a person outside the team who is apostolically gifted and is willing to pray for an impartation of that gift to your leader, with the leader's permission, of course. There is no rule against such support coming from outside the team, although the leader will still of course have to be the one to do the actual leading.

4. <u>"What if I'm just not gifted for the role I've been placed in?"</u> This is a variation of the first three questions above, and it has essentially the same answer. If you cannot change the role to which you've been assigned, do the best you can to fulfill

---

84   "Heal the sick, raise the dead, cleanse those who have leprosy, drive out demons. Freely you have received, freely give." (Matthew 10:8)

it anyway, asking the Holy Spirit for help. It may take some effort, some extra energy, but it's only for a season. You will learn and grow from the experience. At the same time, try to determine whether and how your main gifts can still be used to benefit the team or group, without stepping on anyone's toes.

5. <u>"I've been placed in an apostolic role, but I'm in over my head. Now what?"</u> Don't be afraid to ask for help. Here's a story of what *should* happen if you do.

    When we were preparing to open test markets for L'eggs® pantyhose, we needed to find managers for each market. Bob Engle, head of our direct-to-store distribution department and a veteran of big company distribution operations, had the job of staffing and overseeing this aspect of the business. For the Kansas City test market, he selected "Jim." Jim was a young production supervisor in the pantyhose mill. He was smart, had an understanding of logistics and had demonstrated some leadership skills. His job would be to go to Kansas City, find and lease a warehouse, take delivery of a small fleet of Ford Econoline vans specially fitted with racks to our specifications, recruit a clerical staff and a team of route sales representatives, take delivery and oversee the assembly and placement of our proprietary displays in dozens of supermarkets and drug stores, and then manage the operation. He had to work on a tight timetable to make sure the availability of product in the stores and the ability to restock the displays matched the start of our advertising campaign.

    After Jim had been in Kansas City a short time, Bob received an unexpected call from him. "I desperately need your help," Jim said. "We're working day and night, but I think I'm in over my head here. I don't really know what I'm doing, and if I don't get help quickly we're going to blow the timetable and have a disaster."

Bob and a couple of other people from headquarters immediately hopped on a plane to Kansas City. It took some effort, but things got straightened out and the launch happened on time.

Back at headquarters, Bob was asked, "Aren't you going to fire Jim?" "Fire him? Are you kidding?" Bob responded. "It was my mistake to send him out there, not his. Jim had the wisdom and the courage to realize he had a problem, think of the company ahead of his personal reputation, ask for help, and then stick with it until the problem was solved. That's the kind of people we need around here!"

Jim came back home, almost to a hero's welcome, and resumed his career with the company in manufacturing roles, eventually becoming a fine manager.

Although not cut out for the branch manager's job, Jim demonstrated the important apostolic characteristics of putting the needs of the company ahead of his own, recognizing the need for skills to complement his own, and staying with the assignment long enough to see it through to successful completion. So can you.

6. "What if, based on a careful assessment and/or sad experience, I simply don't think I fit anywhere on this team?" There is no shame in asking to be reassigned or unassigned, or even for resigning if that is an option you can live with. But if you are truly stuck, make the best of it. Again, it's only for a season. Things *will* change.

CAUTION: GIFTING DOES NOT EQUAL QUALIFICATION AND CHARACTER

While we are here talking about hiring or selecting people for various positions in an organization or on a team, this is a good place to interject that it's not smart to select people based solely on their gifts.

You must first determine, "Is the candidate *qualified* to do the job (based on experience, maturity, skills [gifts themselves do not equal skills], etc.), or can he/she be trained to do it in the required timeframe?" and "Is the candidate a person of such *character* (integrity, moral standards, maturity, reputation, etc.) as to be trustworthy in the position?"

You don't hire a financial director simply because she's prophetic. You don't want a marketing person simply because he's evangelistic. You don't hire an office manager simply based on her faith declaration (assuming that's important to you) and the fact that she has worked as a filing clerk in an office a long time and has a gift for teaching others how to do that job, even though teaching is an important gift for a manager. You want to know if she can actually manage, give direction, keep multiple balls in the air, etc., or that she has the potential to learn if you happen to have the time to train her. You want to know she won't steal the office supplies and open up another business at home with them. If those things check out, then the other factors may be considered.

To their chagrin, many Christian employers have hired someone based more or less solely on the fact that the applicant was a Christian, only to find out too late he wasn't really qualified to do the work or couldn't be trusted because of some character weakness that could not be corrected on the job. (Guess what: Christians aren't perfect just because they're Christians.) I'm sure it's happened in other organizations as well, where faith, ethnicity, political persuasion, or giftedness in some particular area alone were deemed very important and were considered above qualifications and character.

Further development of the topics of qualification and character are outside the scope of this book. However, don't get so caught up in what this book is telling you about giftedness and how to identify and apply it that you lose your perspective on this important caveat.

ACTIVATION EXERCISES

1. If you haven't already done so, meditate on the suggested daily prayer below (and in Appendix B). Is it meaningful to you, and do you think it applies in your situation?

2. Putting in mind an organization you are leading or are about to lead, or one you are a part of, go through the steps outlined above, at least in "rough draft" or "first pass" form, to begin to get a feel for what you will be doing when you are ready or called to apply five-fold leadership for real.

A DAILY APOSTOLIC PRAYER

Lord, I acknowledge and thank You that all authority comes from You. I thank you for those in authority over me, and I ask You to bless them, in Jesus' name. Thank you for this assignment You have given me for or concerning (organization, endeavor, task, responsibility, etc.). Now I ask You to help me with it.

Right now I claim the promise of 2 Chronicles 7:14, bowing before You, seeking Your face and asking You to show me any ways from which I need to repent. (Pause and listen) I do repent of _____ and ask for Your forgiveness and for Your healing touch upon me, upon those I work with, and upon the endeavor You have called me to.

Lord, please bless (organization or endeavor) and bring a spirit of unity to it. Show me who I need to be for everyone involved, and show them, and me, who they need to be for me. Thank You for showing me who has the gift of prophecy or discernment, who has the gift of pastoring or compassion, the gift of teaching, the gift of evangelism or persuasion, and the gifts of administration and serving and any other gifts according to how these gifts are needed to carry out the work You have planned for this endeavor. Thank You for showing me how to help each of these people to walk out the destiny You have for them. I pray for wisdom, vision, revelation, plans, provision, courage and perseverance.

Thank You for showing us how to work together in unity according to Ephesians 4:11–16 so that the whole organization grows and builds itself up in love as each part does its work according to Your purposes.

Thank you for the success You have promised with this assignment. I give You all the glory for it.

In Jesus' name I pray. Amen.

CHAPTER 13

APPLICATION HANDBOOK, PART 2 – GUIDELINES FOR BALANCED OPERATION

The Bible doesn't tell us how to apply the five-fold leadership model in terms of structure and protocol. That is probably a good thing because otherwise we would treat it as a sacred recipe and become very pharisaical about it, never deviating from the prescribed way. God knows there are different forms that work for different situations, and He allows us to figure them out with Holy Spirit guidance, or at least by trial and error.

Scholars can tell us the protocol for Sabbath day meetings in the Old Testament synagogues and even for the meetings of the priests and other leaders, including administrators, behind the scenes. All we really know from the Bible about the structure and practices of the early New Testament churches is:

a. There were elders appointed or elected by apostolic figures.

b. There were prophets and teachers among the elders along with apostles in the church at Antioch (Acts 13:1–3), a forerunner and possibly a model for other New Testament churches, and it is likely there were elders with pastoral, evangelistic, teaching and other gifts.

c. Questions and problems that arose were thoroughly and prayerfully discussed by the leadership after inviting all appropriate input before decisions were taken.[85]

Again, scholars could tell us, but I presume at least among the Jewish believers their initial meetings were patterned after those in the synagogues since that is what they knew. But even those protocols and agendas may have been tempered by the egalitarianism they practiced in the earliest days where the believers shared their possessions with one another according to need (See Acts 4:32–37.). It is exciting to imagine them reading from the Scrolls with new understanding of the Trinity and of the prophecies about the coming Messiah who came!

But what about the Gentile churches? And how did the new Way and new understanding impact the believers' behavior in the marketplace? They didn't yet have the New Testament to guide them, only the unfolding teachings and examples of Peter, Paul and other apostles, prophets, evangelists, pastors, and teachers that they witnessed or heard about from letters and from stories passed by word of mouth.

What were their organizations like? What were their decision making processes, in church and in commerce and

---

85   The decision process of replacing Judas with Matthias (Acts 1:15–26), the decision to appoint deacons to relieve the Apostles of the day-to-day burdens of service (Acts 6:1–6), and how the leaders at Jerusalem dealt with the issue of the Holy Spirit falling upon the Gentiles at Cornelius' house (Acts 10, 11) and the question of whether Gentile believers should be circumcised (Acts 15:1–32) are excellent examples.

social life? How widely did their practices vary from church to church? It would be foolish to use the answers to these questions as templates for our own practices. Every situation is different. Every organization has different needs. All I would say is, whatever you do, do it with five-fold in mind.

Having said that, I do have some suggestions you should consider for governance and organization structure, protocol for meetings, and the care and maintenance of five-fold leadership operations in your organization.

GOVERNANCE AND STRUCTURE

Ephesians 4:11–16 is the plan of five-fold governance or leadership. The leadership team should be made up of, or, if the team is small, have access to, mature people with identified five-fold gifting. These are the "elders" of your organization. The structure is up to you.

An obvious suggestion on how to structure is to seek guidance from the five-fold leaders on the team. This is essentially what the apostolic "Level 5" leaders in *Good to Great* did. They got "the right people on the bus" and got organized before they started it down the road. Mostly they organized based on the typical corporate organizational practices of the day, with a typical organization chart, but with variations to suit the specific needs of the company or, in some cases, to fit the particular skills and talents of key leaders or team members.

Structure by Function

The underlying strategy was to organize, or structure, by function. Does the company make consumer products? Then it needs an organization that accommodates manufacturing, which would presumably include buying raw materials and parts, fabricating and assembling, and packaging. It may need market research to analyze and anticipate consumer wants and needs and help determine what product features are important. Does the company want to sell the products? Then it needs salespeople and maybe a marketing department. It needs administrative people, such as accountants, to count the products, pay the vendors, count the sales, receive the money, and so on.

Why does your organization exist? What is your organization trying to do? What are the functions it needs to engage in to accomplish that? We have seen how five-fold gifting often lines up with certain functions, e.g., salesperson = evangelist, human resources = pastoral, and so on. Structure follows function, and they are closely intertwined.

GETTING ORGANIZED – A REITERATIVE PROCESS

With the above in mind, the basic getting organized sequence would be:

1. Establish the five-fold leadership team.

2. Determine the purpose of the organization (which underlies the vision).

3. Identify the functions needed.

4. Decide on structure, and populate the functions with five-fold leaders.

This is a reiterative process. That is, there may be some back-and-forth decisions, or tentative decisions, about purpose, functions needed, and structure as the team comes together and discusses these important issues before everything is finalized. This is not a sign of indecision but rather that the five-fold concept is working as it should. As long as the leadership team members exhibit mutual respect, good and timely decisions will usually be reached by consensus (more on this below).

These steps should be revisited periodically. Organizations and people mature and change, situations change, new problems and opportunities arise, and square pegs may be discovered in round holes after a time in spite of all your efforts (translation: even when applying five-fold, it's still possible to make mistakes, and you shouldn't be afraid of doing so). Keep the "job descriptions" from Chapter 10 close by whenever you revisit your organization structure.

Figure 13–1, below, shows a sample organization chart for a large business. Note the five-fold gifts (as well as administrative) typically found in people occupying certain functional leadership roles. This is just an example and the mix is not always the same in every organization, but this should be helpful in your thinking about how to organize, what to expect, where you might want to place people, and who would form the senior leadership team. (Also refer back to Chapter 12, Next Steps, item 9, "Identify and Form Your Leadership Team.") Note that the leadership team in this example has seven members and the luxury of having four with prophetic gifting, four administrative, three teaching, two pastoral, and two evangelistic along with the one apostolic.

While you're looking at it, see if you can figure out where *you* are, or might best fit, on a chart like this.

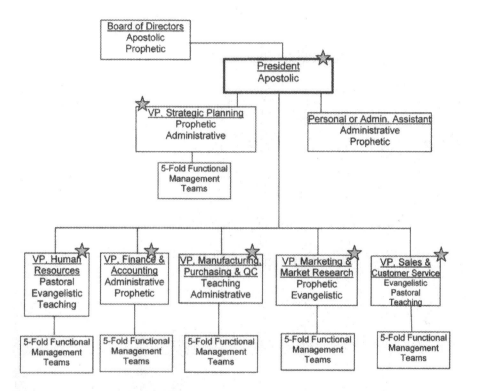

**Figure 13–1: Example Organization Chart Showing
Typical Five-Fold and Functional Relationships**

Protocol: Conducting Meetings[86]

1. <u>The apostle should call the meetings</u>. Even in the case of regularly scheduled meetings, the meeting should have been "called" by the apostle in some way. The leadership grants him or her "calendaring authority." Some organizations' by-laws provide that any member of the ruling board can call a meeting, but even then it usually requires the consent of the senior leader.

2. <u>The apostle sets the agenda</u>, but only after seeking input from the other members of the team. She may delegate the development of the agenda and the seeking of team input to it, but the final agenda is set by her.

3. <u>The apostle should lead the meeting</u>. Note, there is a difference between "leading" and "chairing" a meeting. In the case of one board I know of, the apostolic leader may ask another leader to chair the meeting because of that person's administrative gift and because it frees him from concerns over protocol to concentrate on the major issues being discussed. Even then, however, there is no doubt about who is really leading.

4. <u>Make sure each of the five-fold heart motivations is heard and honored</u>. Draw people out if necessary over every issue. Ask what people are sensing in general or from the Holy Spirit. Aim for balanced five-fold representation.

5. <u>Decide by consensus</u>. Although putting certain things to a vote may be required in your by-laws, that should be thought of as merely "making official" a decision reached

---

86 Much of the discussion in points 1–5 was inspired by the excellent examination of church eldership team function in Chapter Three of Mark and Patti Virkler's *How to Build a Winning Team,* © 1992, Communion with God Ministries. It applies to all five-fold organizations and can be adapted to any size group.

by whatever way you choose. A five-fold team is not a democracy. Nor is it a dictatorship where the apostolic leader rules. If there is balanced five-fold representation, and if there is clear understanding of the situation and the vision for the organization (including mission, objectives, philosophy and strategy), which should be the case if those have previously been established according to five-fold principles, then reaching consensus, i.e., unity, should not be too difficult. If it is elusive, pray, wait, even fast, and come together again. The Session at my former church had a requirement of unanimity on all votes. More than once we literally got down on our knees during a meeting to pray for guidance. You can too.

If consensus still isn't there, maybe it is an issue God doesn't think needs to be decided right now. His timing is always best.

Notice I equated consensus with unity. That is not the same thing as unanimity. A requirement of unanimity implies some degree of control or coercion, and I am not in favor of it, even though I cited it in my Session example above. With consensus there is true unity of spirit and purpose with no violation of free will.

Sometimes, during the process of achieving consensus, one or more individuals who disagree with the decision being proposed will choose to come into agreement with it even if not entirely convinced. Often this is actually a courageous act, not merely an accession by someone who has no backbone. After being heard on the matter and carefully assessing all the arguments, they choose to set their point of view aside for the good of the group. This is a perfect example of other-centered love in action.

I am certainly not saying that servanthood or other-centered love requires us to mindlessly defer to one another all the time. An Alphonse and Gaston routine will lead nowhere.

Disagreement is allowed, even welcomed, and all that is required is a mutually respectful sifting through of the various points of view and alternatives.

Once consensus is reached and a decision is made, everybody must get behind it and support it. That is unity. Otherwise, it is a sure sign that consensus has not really been reached, and seeds of division will sprout.

6. Occasional unilateral rule may be okay. This is dangerous territory, but here goes. Sometimes an apostle may have to make a decision and everybody just needs to go along with it. I'm not talking about an emergency where there is no time to get five-fold input. Usually, there are provisions for that in by-laws or operating protocols previously established under five-fold governance. I'm talking about a case where the apostle feels so strongly that he has heard clear guidance from the Holy Spirit that he asks for a temporary suspension of normal procedures and, after explaining this to the leadership team, says something like, "I just need you to trust me and go along with me this time."

Why would the Holy Spirit seemingly disrespect the five-fold governance model in some cases? I don't know, but I have seen it twice, both times in the same organization but separated by several years. My suspicion is that in the particular organization where this occurred, five-fold governance was not really operating fully in the first place and the apostle didn't quite trust the team and/or felt the team didn't fully trust him, so he needed to plow ahead with the decisions, which were in fact major ones. In the first case everything worked out fine, and in the second things eventually worked out after a fair amount of drama. Neither case was a comfortable situation for anyone.

I won't rule out the possibility that this can be okay in rare instances, but if it does come up, I believe it can be taken as a sign that the five-fold leadership practice in your organization may not be as healthy as it could be and needs to be prayerfully addressed.

DECISION-MAKING: CONSENSUS AND THE AUTHORITY OF THE APOSTLE

The decision-making process is one of the trickiest and possibly the most controversial subjects we have to deal with here. Above, I've said it should be done by consensus except in very rare instances where the apostolic figure must make a unilateral ruling.

In our culture, decisiveness among leaders is highly valued. We think management by consensus is for pantywaists and takes too long. In business, circumstances change so fast that quick decisions must be made, and there is no time for useless debate, although at least it is recognized that gathering as much information and input from others as possible in the time allowed is useful. Even *Star Trek's* Captain Jean Luc Picard asked his officers to suggest alternatives before action was taken when the warlike Romulans were only seconds away from blowing the Enterprise to kingdom come. And the Japanese, famous for cutting-edge manufacturing efficiency, still find time for *nemawashi*.[87] The trouble arises when debate and discussion degenerate into argument or confusion due to a lack of leadership or when an apostolic figure exercises dominance, which is contrary to Jesus' instructions for leadership (Matthew 20:25–26) because it ignores the aspect of servanthood.

---

87   The process the Japanese call "*nemawashi*" literally means "digging around in the roots" of an issue and is loosely translated in the business world as "laying the groundwork" for a big decision. It can take time because everyone involved is given a chance to weigh in, turning it over and over until consensus is reached, and often the responses are indirect especially if they go against whatever may be the prevailing thought. This drives decisive Westerners crazy. Nevertheless, I believe God's thought process is more Asian than Western, and we should try to stick to His. Recall the discussion of Greek versus Hebrew mind-sets in Chapter 2.

James' Example

If a decision is to be by consensus, but an apostolic leader is in charge, then what does that look like? A good example is the way Peter, and especially James, demonstrated leadership when the believers at Jerusalem wanted Gentile Christians to be circumcised according to the law of Moses.

Acts 15:5–24 describes the meeting of the apostles and elders to discuss this question of doctrine. First, Peter argues that since God has clearly already welcomed Gentiles into the faith by grace (a reference to his experience at Cornelius' house, and subsequent evidence), there is no reason to add the requirement of circumcision. Barnabas and Paul then report how God has been performing miraculous signs and wonders through the Gentile believers, and Simon reminds the assembly that God's acceptance of the Gentiles was prophesied (Amos 9:11–12).

At that point, James speaks up authoritatively, yet not in a domineering way. "Brothers, listen to me," he says. He gets their attention. They know he has something important to say. It could be the answer they are seeking. He quotes the prophecy of Amos and then says, "It is my judgment, therefore, that we should not make it difficult for the Gentiles who are turning to God" (v. 19). Decision offered. No one objects. Decision made. The rest of the discussion centers on the simple matter of how to carry out the decision by telling the Gentiles the good news.

Notice James does not say, "It is my decision," but rather, "It is my *judgment*." He does not cut off further debate, but his words carry authority and everyone knows it is time for a decision and this is the right one. That is consensus.

Maintaining Apostolic Philosophy

Just because you have a five-fold team in place and have intentioned to apply the five-fold leadership principles throughout your organization doesn't mean it will work like a perpetual motion machine. It needs fuel and maintenance, just like anything else that is alive and growing. It is the apostle's role to see that these are supplied. Constant prayer and seeking of the Holy Spirit for yourself and the organization should go without saying. Take another look at the crafted prayer at the end of Chapter 13 or in Appendix B. Beyond that, let me offer these suggestions:

1. <u>Treat all others with love, honor and respect</u>, not only for their gifts, but mostly for who they are in Christ. My friend Steve Sizemore, an elder at Grace Church, shared with a study group this entry from his daily journaling and gave me permission to share it here. It beautifully sums up the apostolic heart attitude we all need to have, regardless of which five-fold role we are in.

   <u>Question</u>: Lord, how would you like for me to show greater honor, respect and love toward my spouse, my children, and/ or my friends you have given to me?

   <u>Answer</u>: Accept and love others for who they are and where they are. Doing so will open the door to their heart for a more intimate relationship. As you do so, your influence will grow. You will not need to offer advice because they will be asking for it. Then, that which I have invested into you can be given. Remember the saying "Preach the gospel and if necessary use words." That is what I am talking about. Live by my Spirit; be resourced by the fruit production in your life. And that fruit will produce more fruit. Keep your heart clear of offence. This will keep the fruit flowing. The greatest way for you to honor and show respect is releasing your expectations of others… allow them to flow and grow in Me.

   Refer to Romans 12, reprinted in Appendix A, which goes into this even more deeply. We'll come back to it later.

2. <u>At the same time, look for opportunities to help people rise</u>

to a higher functioning level. Not only are we interested in equipping people to do the right jobs and to do their jobs better, but also we want wherever possible to help them to become qualified for even more responsibility. The teacher's goal should always be to produce students who are as qualified or better qualified than even the teacher. It's about transforming disciples (students) into apostles in the sense that they can then be sent forth either within the growing enterprise or outside it to reproduce themselves yet again, and so on. This obviously benefits the enterprise, and moreover, it is part of helping people to identify and meet their calling and destiny.

3. Set up an accountability group to test your five-fold application periodically. Who should be in this group? Who better than your five-fold leadership team itself? If you have a small team, say up to five, the whole group can be the accountability group. If the team is larger, then select from the most senior and mature among them, and probably limit it to five or six. You might consider rotating the membership, however, maybe on an annual basis. You might also consider inviting someone from outside the team or organization who may bring an objective perspective, but it should be someone mature, well-versed in five-fold principles and familiar with your situation.

The purpose of the accountability group is to perform an occasional reality check on how well you are applying five-fold leadership. You should do this no matter how large or small your organization is.

Checklist of questions for the accountability group
a. Does everybody on the leadership team understand the five-fold concept?
b. Is there understanding and buy-in from the rest of the organization? What about any new people?

c. Do any of the five-fold leaders feel they are not being heard from enough or that others are heard from too often (candidness will be important), whether it is them personally or from other parts of the organization where five-fold resides?

d. Is five-fold being included and experienced at every level of the organization that you intend it to be?

e. How well are the "saints" being equipped to do what they need to do? How do you know, i.e., what measures or benchmarks are you using to monitor this?

f. What results, positive or negative, can you point to that are attributable to operating with five-fold?

g. Is there unity of purpose in the organization? If not, what is blocking it?

h. Does everybody in the organization know what their job is, what they are supposed to be doing and how they contribute to the whole?

i. Do most people seem to have some idea of their purpose, calling, and destiny in life?

j. How many are growing in their jobs to the point where they might be ready for promotion or new challenges that will stretch them even further?

k. Is there strife in the organization that goes beyond the normal, healthy tensions between different heart motivations and different departmental objectives? If so, why, and how should it be addressed so that unity and alignment can be restored?

l. Is the organization growing—not necessarily in terms of financial size, although that's important for a business, or in numbers of people, which is okay if it is the result of or in anticipation of real business growth—but in maturity, understanding, love, and the ability to apply five-fold?

I'm taking most of these questions right out of Ephesians 4:11–16. Your team can brainstorm for additional questions that may pertain more directly to your needs and situation.

Don't expect all of these questions to be answered favorably after only a short time of practicing five-fold. In most cases, employing five-fold requires a major paradigm shift and the establishing of entirely new thought habits, a renewing of the minds involved. It's a process. Stick with it.

How often to meet?

At first, you might convene the accountability group once a month. Later, maybe you will feel comfortable going to a quarterly or semi-annual schedule. It is probably unwise to let it go beyond six months, however. It needs regular maintenance after you establish it. Times and situations change, and your team must adapt. Roles may need to change. New people may come into the organization. Some people may transfer or drop out. The meeting of one set of objectives results in new ones being established. The entrepreneurial person or team who started the company successfully may not have the needed skills to manage it when it becomes mature, so a new team must be installed. (Obviously, that big a change can't be dealt with in one meeting of the accountability group, but it will certainly be a topic of discussion from which will come needed input to those deciding on the changes necessary.)

Consider combining these meetings with the periodic discussions that revisit the "getting organized" sequence as recommended in Structure by Function, above.

Little foxes creep into the best-tended vineyards when the superintendent sleeps. Constant Holy Spirit led refreshment will be needed.

ACTIVATION EXERCISES

1. Do you think these steps and advice are really practical? Can you see yourself leading or participating in them in your organization? What else would have to take place before that could happen? List your concerns.

2. Does this help you in your understanding of consensus decision making? Can you think of examples where you have seen this happen?

3. What other accountability group checklist questions can you think of? List them.

4. Are you excited to begin trying these guidelines in your organization? What additional guidelines can you think of? List them. (Pretend you are helping me write the next edition of this book.)

5. Take time now to read Romans 12 (Appendix A). We'll return to it later too.

CHAPTER 14

Application Handbook, Part 3 – Apostolic Responsibility for Destiny

The idea of prophesying over someone to help that person perceive his or her calling and destiny may seem daunting. Also, it may seem like meddling in someone's personal life, which, in a way, it is. Well, not "meddling" really. More like assisting. Meddling means intruding without permission, and that is not what this is about. This is about helping a person close the gap between how he sees himself and how God sees him. It may be how God sees him now or it may be how God sees him in the future (the "destiny" part of it).

Gideon's Example

When the angel of the Lord encountered Gideon hiding in the winepress, he declared, "The Lord is with you, mighty warrior." Gideon argued with the "mighty warrior" part of that because he had a low opinion of himself. Nevertheless, Gideon was willing to listen and ultimately to obey God's instructions for routing the enemy, which caused him to walk into the mighty warrior destiny he had been called to (Judges 6–8).

The angel's declaration was a personal prophecy over Gideon. Such prophecy is always conditional, usually upon what the person does with the word he has heard. Gideon could have ignored it. In doing so he would have violated the conditions God had established for it to come true, namely that Gideon would believe it, align his thoughts with it, and position himself to walk in it. But Gideon also somehow knew enough not to take the prophetic word at face value and instantly believe it. First, he tested it by asking God to give him a sign of its validity, in this case by literally putting out a fleece (Judges 6:17–22). Only when God had satisfied Gideon that the word was truly from Him did Gideon accept it. And God was not unhappy that Gideon wanted to be sure.

Cultural Bias against "Getting Involved"

Over the past 100 years there have been varying opinions about whether employers should get involved in the personal lives of their employees, and if so, how. The prevailing thought, however, was that it was probably a bad idea.

That began to change in the 1980s when the "Total Quality Management (TQM) Movement" was launched. TQM was led by the likes of W. Edwards Deming (*Deming's 14 Points for Management*), J.M Juran (*Juran on Leadership for Quality: An Executive Handbook),* and Philip Crosby (*Quality is Free*). The key TQM concepts required managers to get to know their people better, to identify and understand their strengths and weaknesses, and (gasp) to give them the freedom, or "empowerment," to team with each other to try to solve their own work problems and improve efficiency not by working harder but by coming up with better ways of doing things.

This involved employees and management working together to develop processes, systems, and policies instead of simply having management dictate them. It could be described as "holistic" in the sense that it began to recognize that employees were capable of viewing the company as organic, like a body, an entity made up of components which, when properly related, could make the whole effectively greater than the sum of its parts (very much like what is described in Ephesians 4:16. Imagine that!).

Along with training in TQM came an emphasis on work/life balance, or integrating work and non-work life. But even in the 1980s and 1990s there was still a reluctance to get "too involved" in employees' personal lives. That reluctance is still there, but if five-fold is to work best then we must overcome that reluctance at least to the extent of helping people to see who they are as God sees them.

Your Responsibility Today, as It Was from the Beginning

A critical part of five-fold leadership's equipping responsibility is to help people find and walk in their calling "according to His purpose" and to help them identify and move ever toward their destiny on this earth.

"And we know that in all things God works for the good of those who love him, who have been called according to his purpose" (Romans 8:28).

"For we are God's workmanship, created in Christ Jesus to do good works, which God prepared in advance for us to do" (Ephesians 2:10).

"'For I know the plans I have for you,' declares the Lord, 'plans to prosper you and not to harm you, plans to give you hope and a future'" (Jeremiah 29:11).

The reason this responsibility should be recognized is that when people are doing what they are supposed to be doing, properly equipped and in accord with their gifts, talents, passions, and calling, the enterprise they are engaged in will prosper. If we start with the idea of equipping people via appropriate leadership, as in the Ephesians 4 model, everything else falls into place and the company (the "body") benefits. But if we start with, "How will this benefit the company?" and look at everything from that standpoint, we put the cart before the horse.

Jesus modeled this in the process of equipping His disciples to become apostles. He guided and corrected them according to who they were, and He told them of their destiny and how to position themselves for it.

For us in the five-fold context it starts with the process of helping people to identify their primary gifts and talents. This is not difficult, and some ways of doing it were shown in Chapter 11. This can form a basis for helping to discern one's calling and destiny so that it is more likely the role each person plays in the organization will line up with that. The experience and accomplishments enjoyed in the current season will then be good building blocks for the future realization of one's destiny.

We've all read Proverbs 22:6. "Train up a child in the way he should go, and when he is old he will not turn from it." Did you know this is not just about teaching children politeness and good values? More than that, it is about helping them to discern and position themselves to walk in their destiny, that is, the plans God has for them. That is what's meant by "the way he should go." We think of this, rightly, as primarily a parental responsibility. However, when you are on a five-fold leadership team, and especially if you have the apostolic role, which is father-like, you are acting *in loco parentis*[88] for your team members.

Many people are not even aware that they have a calling and destiny, much less that they can find out what it is. Many think of it in terms of uncontrollable fate, which is the way most religions view it. "Maybe God will smile on me, and maybe He won't. I

---

88   Latin for "in the place of a parent," this term is most often associated with the legal responsibilities of school officials for the well-being of students who are away from home.

pray He will, and I do a lot of stuff to earn His favor, but, really, I don't know what He's going to do with me." They do not realize God sees them in terms of the plans He has for them, that He wants to reveal those plans to them, and that they don't have to do anything to earn what He has for them, only learn how to receive it. What a privilege for you as a leader to help them with this!

None of this absolves each person you work with from having the primary responsibility for seeking God for his or her own calling and destiny, but it is a key role of five-fold leadership to help in this process.

THE PURPOSE OF PROPHECY

Admittedly, the definition of prophecy from the Bible, especially the Amplified version, makes it sound a bit scary: "Interpret the divine will and purpose in inspired preaching and teaching" (1 Corinthians 14:1 and elsewhere). However, hearing the purpose as spelled out in 1 Corinthians 14:3 makes it seem much less so: "But everyone who prophesies speaks to men for their strengthening, encouragement and comfort" (NIV) or "But he that prophesieth speaketh unto men to edification, and exhortation, and comfort" (KJV). I especially like the Amplified Version's language: "But … the one who prophesies…speaks to men for their upbuilding and constructive spiritual progress and encouragement and consolation" (edited). As we saw earlier, too, sometimes these benefits result from a prophecy that confirms something God has said, rather than imparting seemingly new information

What a joy it is for you as a leader to be able to speak words of praise, encouragement and comfort to the people you work with! And by the way, prophesying is not just for angels, lest you be misled by Gideon's experience. All of us can do it.

"HOW DO I PROPHESY OVER SOMEONE?"

All you are really doing is asking God to show you something about the person that will help him to see himself as God sees him, in this case in the context of where he best fits into the organization (body) you are both serving. Although it is supernatural, it is no more so than receiving answers to prayer about anything else. It is not spooky. Therefore, it needn't be frightening either to you or to the person for whom you are seeking a word from God.

Starting out, your biggest concern will probably be whether God will, in fact answer this particular prayer and give you a word. He will, although it may be difficult to "hear" it the first few times. For most people it does take practice, even those who are already gifted to be prophetic. You may fear looking stupid if God doesn't "show up," but if you simply tell yourself and the person you are prophesying over that you are new at it and, "Let's try this together because we know we can trust God," then it will become easier to jump in. When you get a word and you are not sure of it, just say, "I'm not sure," or "I'm not sure what this means, but let me tell you what I think I might be hearing." Remember, it's not you who is "performing," it's God who is answering prayer.

The other person's concern is usually, "Oh, what if God reveals something I don't want anyone to know about?" God sometimes does allow a prophetic person to "read your mail" in detail. But even then, we need to understand the concept of "how God sees you." Love sees only the good and acts only for good (1 Corinthians 13). As a Christian, your sin was washed away by Jesus' sacrifice on the Cross. God, therefore, does not see you as bad. He sees only the good, whether it is in the person you are now or in the one He sees you becoming. At worst (which is actually best), he sees areas of opportunity where the Holy Spirit has not yet dealt with you about something that could be improved. When that is identified and addressed, you are strengthened. The confirming of the good things in you is also strengthening, encouraging and comforting. All three are helpful and positive, and they contain nothing to be afraid of.

"What Do I Do?"

It is usually better to prophesy with the person present, but it is not a requirement. In some instances it may not even be possible, especially if you are in an environment where the prophetic is not accepted.

In either case, the process is essentially the same. First, get quiet before the Lord, eliminating distractions that may prevent you from hearing from Him. Then, with your focus on God (or Jesus), ask Him silently or aloud what He wants to say to you about the person. Wait for an answer, which could come in any of several forms, usually depending on how you normally hear from the Lord. It could be an audible voice or a "knowing" in your spirit that wasn't there a moment before. It could be a vision or a picture, or maybe a word or words written on the screen of your mind. It could be a Scripture passage that comes to mind. Or it could be nothing more than an impression of a feeling, a word that comes to mind, or a mood you begin to sense or feel.

Whatever it is, the next step is to ask God what it means, unless that is already very clear. If your impression is a vision of the person sitting at the controls of an airplane, for example, and the person is not a pilot, you need to know if that should be taken literally or whether it is symbolic for the possibility that the person will become the head of a successful international business or ministry. If the impression is merely a color, like red, or a feeling, like joy, you may want to ask the Lord for more or ask why He is showing you that and what it might mean.

Sometimes, especially if the meaning is not clear to you, you might ask the person if it means anything to him. "Ted, all I'm getting is the color red and then it sort of turns to black. Does that mean anything to you?" God can just as easily speak to Ted as to you and in fact sometimes wants Ted to hear it directly from Himself and is using you as the catalyst to get the conversation going. Ted may say it doesn't mean anything to him. In that case, both of you should just note it and put it aside. Maybe your impression was wrong, or maybe it's something God will choose to reveal more about later. On the other hand, Ted may say, "Yes!

My department has been going over budget and losing money for a long time. We're always 'in the red.' I've been praying about it, and maybe God is saying we're going to 'go into the black' soon and start being a contributor to the company instead of a drain." Remember, you may not yet know for sure if this is true, but since in this case it's a good thing, you can bless it by thanking God for the word of encouragement and then praying that it will come to pass.

That encouragement alone may stimulate Ted to open up new ways of thinking about his responsibilities as head of his department and seek new tactics or strategies for its financial management that he may have been too discouraged to think of or hear from God about before. God is answering his prayers, and Ted is walking toward his destiny as a successful manager who has prophetic gifting.

And as for you, you have learned something about Ted that will help you, the apostolic leader of the team he is on, to place him in the best role and support him in it.

"What Should Ted Do Now?"

Like Gideon, the person receiving the prophetic word needs to test it before accepting it right away at face value. He should ask: Does the word come from someone I trust and who has given valid words to others that I know of? Does it line up with Scripture? Does it seem to be consistent with the spiritual path I have already been on for some time? Does it line up with my interests, passions, gifting and talent, at least to the extent that I understand those things? When I share it with my spouse, trusted friends, elders in my church, or my pastor, does it seem to them as if it is from God and makes sense for my life? Is it consistent with other prophetic words I may have received over some period of time? When I pray and ask God to explain or confirm the word, what does He say? If the answers to most (even if not all) of these questions, especially the last one, seem to agree at least generally or directionally, then the word is probably valid.

"What If I Don't Hear Anything?"

If it is comfortable for Ted, it could be very helpful to engage him in a conversation about some of the questions discussed above. What are his passions, the things he really enjoys doing and gets the most satisfaction from? What are his gifts and talents? Are there areas where he thinks he has seen God at work in his life already? What were these "spiritual markers," and do they seem to be milestones on a path or direction that God has put him on?[89] If so, they could point the way to what God has in store for Ted in the future. Getting Ted to talk about these things will help him to see himself in a different light and to begin to perceive God's plans for him. And, the Holy Spirit may speak to you or Ted during the conversation.

At the very least, if you are truly not hearing an answer from the Holy Spirit when you pray for a word for someone, you can "punt" by changing your prayer to, "Lord, please show (Name) his calling and destiny. Show him his heart's desire, if he doesn't know for sure what that is. Or put a desire in his heart that lines up well with Your will and plans for him. Then grant him that desire." But punting won't help you develop this important skill. Don't let discouragement stop you from continuing to pray for words from the Lord for the people you work with.

You shouldn't necessarily expect instant results when you begin the process of learning to prophesy. It is just that, a process. Even for those who "get it right away" it takes time to further develop the ability to hear more and more clearly from God. As with

---

89   Henry Blackaby summarizes this concept: "When God gets ready for you to take a new step or direction in His activity, it will always be in sequence with what He has already been doing in your life." See his excellent discussion of spiritual markers in *Experiencing God: Knowing and Doing the Will of God*," by Henry T. Blackaby and Claude V. King, © 1990, LifeWay Press, pp.101–104.

building a building, it starts with a good foundation, so don't let discouragement stop you. Ask others who are experienced in this to help guide you in it, or to pray impartations over you for more of this gift. Read about it, study it, and practice as you go. You will hear from Him if you keep practicing. [90]

MY BROTHER'S SERVANT

You may be thinking, "This is too much. Am I my brother's keeper?" No, but you are your brother's servant. When you identify someone's gifting and prayerfully put him or her in the best place on a leadership team or elsewhere in an organization, and help that person grow, you are agreeing with God about His plan for that person's life for that season, and you are contributing to that person's realization of his or her destiny. A team or an organization set up according to the five-fold paradigm is an accountability group. All are accountable to one another for the edification of each other and the organization. As Graham Cooke says, "Accountability is calling people to be who God says they are." As a leader, and as a Christian with the ability to prophesy, you have a responsibility to say, "God, please show me what's going on in that person's life, especially as it pertains to what we are trying to accomplish here, and then tell me what You want (me) to do about it."

Don't think you are left out of this if you are not a Christian.

---

90   To learn how to flow in personal prophecy does take some training and practice, and a comprehensive treatment of the subject is beyond the scope of this book. To learn more, I recommend you find a church that practices this, attend a conference on the prophetic at MorningStar Ministries (Rick Joyner) in Fort Mill, SC (www.morningstarministries.org), attend the annual Voice of the Prophets conference of Global Awakening (Randy Clark, http://globalawakening.com), and/or pick up one or more of these books that demystify prophecy for those new to it and give practical guidelines for how to get started in it: *You May All Prophesy* by Steve Thompson, MorningStar Publications; *User Friendly Prophecy* by Larry Randolph, Destiny Image Publishers, Inc.; *Basic Training for the Prophetic Ministry* by Kris Vallotton , Destiny Image Publishers, Inc.; and *Developing Your Prophetic Gifting* by Graham Cooke, Chosen Books.

At Pentecost, the Spirit was poured out "on *all* people" (Acts 2:17), which means you too have the ability to prophesy, to ask God to give you insight into His plans for a person's life. He will answer you.[91]

Choose Your Burdens

This is not the same thing as "getting too involved in your employees' personal lives." You are not expected to deal with a brother-in-law's gambling problem, fix speeding tickets, or find a nursing home for someone's aging parent. Those are not your burdens; you have enough of your own. They are in a different category from helping people to see and realize their destiny. On the other hand, you can and should show people compassion and understanding and cut them a little slack from time to time if they need it, and of course pray for them.

Summary

The leadership, praying and prophesying over each person, brings a higher level of discernment because of its authority and maturity. The leadership also has the benefit of knowing the vision and plans for the organization which when shared with the people helps them to see how their roles contribute in each progressive season, widening the scope of their own discernment about God's direction for them. Only in this way can unity of faith and purpose be achieved so that each part can know and do its proper work in the building up of the body or organization, thereby to enjoy the full Five-fold Effect.

91　In addition to the books cited in the previous footnote, you can find excellent material from Dr. Mark Virkler's Communion with God Ministries, including the book *4 Keys to Hearing God's Voice* (Destiny Image Publishers, Inc., Shippensburg, PA) and associated workbooks. His emphasis in these teachings is on journaling, which is a great way to start practicing. The principles are entirely applicable to personal prophecy. See www.cwgministries.org/Four-Keys-to-Hearing-Gods-Voice

ACTIVATION EXERCISES

1. If you have prophesied over people in a church setting and this is not new to you, think about how you would start doing it at work. Then, choose someone you work with and privately ask God for a word for that person. When He answers you, write it down and if it seems appropriate to do so, share that word with the person after explaining that you are trying to learn this skill and why. It's okay to be tentative at first, but keep it up. Build on that experience.

2. If the whole idea is new to you, start with a family member or possibly a trusted friend from church and do the same thing. Ask them to do the same for you. Don't be afraid to ask them if the word you had for them means anything to them. This feedback is helpful in the learning process.

3. Keep doing this until you become more and more comfortable with it as your skill at hearing from God increases, which it will.

NOTE: I develop this topic further in an article titled "Apostolic Responsibility for Destiny" in *Aligning with the Apostolic: An Anthology of Apostleship – How Apostles and Apostolic Teams from the Seven Mountains of Culture Are Restoring the Church, Reforming Culture, Transforming Nations, and Advancing the Kingdom of God* compiled and edited by Dr. Bruce Cook, © 2012 Dr. Bruce Cook, Kingdom House, Austin, TX, Volume Four, Section 8, Chapter 51, p. 119.

CHAPTER 15

APPLICATION HANDBOOK, PART 4 – THE LONE RANGER AND (FOUR-FOLD) TONTO

FOR ONE- OR TWO-PERSON SITUATIONS

I can imagine some of you saying, "Walt, what you've written so far is all very well for organizations that have more than a few people in them because surely somewhere in the mix they will be able to identify the necessary five-fold leadership gifts. But you also said this would work even for organizations as small as a two-person committee. How about expanding on that? Oh, and what about somebody who truly works alone? Does that person need five-fold, and how does that work?"

Excellent questions. The short answer is yes, the five-fold leadership principles can and should be applied no matter the size of the organization, even if it seems too small to warrant being called an organization. "No man is an island," said John Donne. In fact, a peninsula is as close as anyone can come to it. In other words, no matter what you are doing, there is always some connection to other people who may be affected by what you do and/or upon whom you can draw for help.

LET'S GO TO THE FIVE-FOLD EFFECT INTERNET CHAT ROOM:

Question: Hi Walt. Eric here. I'm a research scientist wintering at an ice station in Antarctica with...

Answer: Wait a minute; how did you...?

Q: I downloaded your book to my Kindle. The nights are long here (all day long, in fact) and sometimes I need help getting to sleep.

A: Thanks for the encouragement!

Q: No worries. Anyway, I'm here all alone except for my assistant, Igor, who is not prophetic although he thinks he is. Every time a problem comes up he predicts we're going to die.

A: Umm. I perceive he isn't pastoral either. So, how can I help?

Q: I don't mind being apostolic if I have to be, although I'm really better suited as a teacher, but don't you think I'm in kind of an extreme situation?

A: Uh, not at all, Eric. You've taken the first steps, which are to think within the five-fold leadership paradigm, recognize that you are the apostolic figure in your situation, and look around to assess and identify the other five-fold team members. If you're chatting with me, that shows you do have access to outside resources, if only by Internet or satellite communications. So you are not alone.

Q: Yes, but...

A: Who are the people who sent you there? Surely there is a support team back in the States who...

Q: I'm Australian.

A: Oh, sorry. But anyway, surely there is a support team back in Australia that you talk to.

Q: I'm not sure they ever want me back.

A: Umm...

Q: Just kidding, mate.

A: Well stop it. Now think of yourself as having an extended team, if you will, sort of like an extended family. They may not be available for face-to-face interaction with you, but they are accessible. Actually, come to think of it, if you use something like Skype at least some virtual face-to-face communication is possible. Who are the people back home that you can draw on for five-fold input? And don't limit it to the people who sent you. What about family and friends too? Anybody you trust can be a candidate for your extended team. Review the steps in the book, assessing your needs and making a list, and so on. You'll be surprised at how easy it will be. Then start talking to the candidates about the five-fold team concept, using language you think they will understand, and see what happens.

Q: That's very helpful. I'll start today. Thanks.

A: No worries.

Q: Must go now. It's Igor. I wonder what…

(Loss of signal)

Extreme? Not really. The point is, you probably have access to at least an extended team even if you are only a two- or three-person operation and are physically isolated. Fortunately, most of us are not as isolated as Eric. As a last resort, as we saw before, be prepared to fulfill a needed role yourself, with help from the Holy Spirit.

Figure 15–1: Eric and Igor in Antarctica Stay in Touch with the Extended Team in Kingston, Tasmania

"But I Do Work Alone"

Okay, what if you really are the Lone Ranger and work alone? Let's say you are self employed and have a proprietary business where you are the owner, the producer (producing the product or the service by yourself), the salesperson, the bookkeeper, and the janitor, all in one.

Among my friends with their own businesses are:

- A carpenter
- A multi-skilled home improvement contractor
- A guitar teacher and party DJ
- An office space management designer
- A digital photographer and printer of fine art

Each is president of his or her job and has the apostolic role. You may be like them, gifted and skilled in providing the products and services you offer, but maybe you aren't as good at selling or bookkeeping or predicting business trends and shifts in the economy and how those will affect your business. If so, Masked Person, you would benefit from applying the five-fold principles to your enterprise.

You are not Alone

If you're indeed a Lone Ranger like they are, you need a four-fold Tonto, an extended team to help your business thrive and come against the enemy's Butch Cavendish Gang that wants to head you off at the pass. An extended team can be put together from among friends, family, and even customers and suppliers. These people have wisdom and insight into things you may not see because you are not gifted to see them or just because you are too close to your situation to see them objectively. Your spouse is probably a good place to start. He or she is probably gifted in ways that complement your own gift set and undoubtedly has your best interests at heart.

It may seem a strange idea to consider customers and suppliers as potential five-fold team members, but why not? Your success is in their best interest as well as yours. We're all connected and interdependent in this "body" we are trying to build.

Can't afford to hire a salesman? Nevertheless, you still need an evangelist. Who do you know who can build you a great interactive Website? Or show you how to use social media to your advantage, such as a Facebook page, which is free? Are you trying to reach owners of older homes, artists, business owners, young budding musicians, etc.? Who has contacts in those worlds and the winsome personality to spread the word about you, or at least make introductions, assuming you don't?

Often you can find people willing to lend you their services and advice free of charge or at very low rates as an act of friendship and support. Some of them may be willing to "invest" by charging low rates now because they hope you will become a steady and valuable customer later when you become a greater success.

Maybe there are high school or college students willing to help because they want to learn about your business or hope you will hire them someday (but don't give them unrealistic hopes or promises). Maybe they are retired and instead of just playing golf or becoming couch potatoes they want to keep their hands in and their minds sharp with a challenging assignment that they don't need to be paid for. (At least take them to dinner occasionally, not just for coffee at Starbucks.)

Are there trade organizations, local business associations, the Chamber of Commerce, or civic clubs you can join for networking and where you may find advocates (evangelistic), people willing to give you advice or leads (prophetic), people to compare notes with (pastoral), people who can show you new or different techniques (teaching) that will improve your skills at what you do? Think creatively about these questions. Ask the Holy Spirit to bring names and ideas to mind. Then make a list and jot down a plan to pursue these ideas and these people. Think of it as making legal demands and withdrawals from a five-fold resource bank that you yourself have founded, as shown in Figure 15–2.

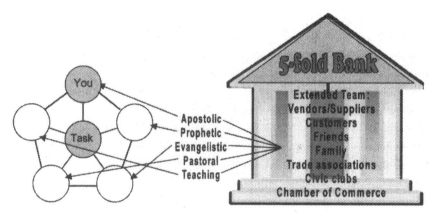

Figure 15–2: The Lone Ranger (You) Makes Withdrawals from the Five-fold Resource Bank to Form an Extended Team

I almost hate to use the word, but be religious about it. Be intentional. Don't put it off, and don't do it halfway. If you don't feel you have the discipline or the administrative skill, ask somebody you trust and respect to help you with the plan. With that step alone you will already be applying five-fold. It's not so hard.

"I've Tried All That and My Team is Still Incomplete"

You're not off the hook.

I'm reminded of Lt. Commander Data from the TV series, *Star Trek: The Next Generation*. A sophisticated android (It was politically incorrect to call him a robot.), Data had what you might call a Pinocchio complex. He constantly wanted to become more like a human, but the main thing he lacked was emotion. Whenever Lt. Commander Geordi La Forge would install the infamous "emotion chip" into Data's positronic brain, Data would drive everybody crazy with mood swings, uncontrolled outbursts of joy and grief, and clumsy, ill-timed attempts at humor, endangering ship and crew but delightfully entertaining the audience. I'm chuckling as I contemplate Geordi installing a "prophetic chip" in Data's brain. Of course that, combined with the emotion chip, would have made his character too much like that of Lt. Commander Scott, the engineering officer in the original *Star Trek* series: "She canna take any more, Captain! She's gonna blow!" It's a wonder Scotty didn't get transferred to Antarctica.

Where am I going with this? It's a stretch, maybe, but like Data trying to become a human, we are humans becoming more like Christ. The difference is that we have the "Holy Spirit chip." And it works perfectly. Jesus was and is the complete five-fold minister and leader. When we see and speak His promises, and follow His plans for us, we are being transformed into His likeness (2 Corinthians 3:18). We can even call things that are not as though they are (Romans 4:17). So if you are truly stuck for a complete five-fold team to work with you, you can still rely on the Holy Spirit to guide you in the areas that are lacking, if you ask Him. And as I keep saying, don't be afraid to fulfill a needed role yourself if you must. Ask Him to re-wire you with an impartation of the gift or gifts needed for the task at hand.

Or, seek out people you trust who have a substantial measure of the gift or gifts you lack, and ask them to pray prayers of impartation over you. The Holy Spirit can be a Divine usher, directing to you the people you need, and you to people who need you. You can ask such people to pray for impartations over your team members too, in order to help gain access to all five gifts for the team. (Again, see Appendix C for a more detailed discussion of impartation of spiritual gifts.)

Consider nurturing your imparted gifts through seminars, books, or professional organizations. The Internet is a rich source of information and training materials as well.

In all times, pray for His wisdom and revelation, and listen for His voice to answer you. Share what He is telling you with the team members you do have, and others whom you respect as spiritually mature, for confirmation and interpretation. He will meet your needs.

NOT A SILVER BULLET

Five-fold is not a Lone Ranger silver bullet that solves all your problems in one shot. It is complex and has many moving parts, and it requires training and practice to become proficient. However, once you and your organization purpose to look at things through the lens of the five-fold paradigm, the rest will begin to fall into place for you. When The Five-fold Effect begins to be felt, it will be as if your organization is "shot from guns."[92]

A MULLIGAN FOR FRED

Remember Fred, the failed would-be cupcake mogul from

---

92 Unfortunately for my purposes, "The Lone Ranger" was sponsored by General Mills, not Quaker, the makers of Quaker Puffed Wheat and Quaker Puffed Rice, the cereals "shot from guns."

Chapter 8? Now, keeping in mind the application of the five-fold gifts, let's see how things might have turned out if there were mulligans in real life like there are in a friendly game of golf. By way of illustrating the application of the principles we have just learned, let's give Fred a second chance.

ACTIVATION EXERCISES

1. Have you found yourself and your situation in the book, not necessarily in this chapter? (Actually, you may be in more than one situation to which these guidelines can be applied.) If so, do you feel ready to tackle applying five-fold to it? If not, what is still missing for you before you feel you are ready? How could you bridge the gap?

2. Have you already tried applying five-fold to an organizational situation? Have you seen any results? How do you feel about it?

3. If your situation is not addressed here, are there any that come close? Is it possible for you to translate them to your situation? Try it.

4. Discuss your answers to #1 and #2 with someone else, and see if you can come up with solutions to your concerns that will allow you to proceed with confidence.

5. If you are a Lone Ranger, review the specific suggestions in this chapter and list the ones that may work for you. Add to the list any others that come to mind in your process of thinking about these. Use them to build a simple plan of action.

6. If you are still hesitant, start anyway, even if you are more comfortable starting small, taking baby steps, until you have the confidence to act more boldly. Then boldly go where no new apostle has gone before!

CHAPTER 16

"Fred Takes the Cake"

Fred and Judy sat in their kitchen sipping lemonade while a pizza warmed in the oven. They'd spent an interesting afternoon looking at several places where they might locate the new business they were planning to start.

"I like the one at the corner of Baker Boulevard and 13th Street," said Fred excitedly. "It's been vacant for a year so we can get the lease cheap, with the furniture and fixtures thrown in. And there's a lot of traffic there, with the McDonald's and the gas station across the street and the auto parts store next door. What do you think?"

"I have to agree about the traffic," said Judy, "but there aren't very many parking spaces, and it's a tight squeeze getting in and out of the parking lot. I'm not sure I like putting a bakery next to an auto parts store, and the fact it's been vacant for so long might be telling us something too."

The oven timer chimed, and Judy rose to take out the pizza. She put a generous slice on each of their plates and sat down again.

Fred had been a senior machinist at a manufacturing plant in town. He was the best, supervising a crew of three, tackling even the most challenging assignments to build, remodel or repair everything from the smallest to the largest of the equipment. His team had the best safety record of any in the company as well as the lowest downtime for repairs, so production was rarely interrupted by equipment problems. "It's all about good maintenance and planning ahead," Fred always told his crew, and they took it to heart.

Alas, after 25 years, Fred's job was exported, and he was forced to take early retirement. It was an attractive severance and pension package, however, and after a lot of thought and prayer he chose to take it as a lump sum. He'd always dreamed of being his own boss, and maybe this was a chance to start a business.

"Hmmm," said Fred, pondering Judy's answer. "You're probably right, but I sure like the idea of being on 'Baker' Boulevard with a bakery."

"That's cute all right, but the landlord wants a two-year lease," said Judy. "Don't you think that's a little risky for a start-up? Or, to be more positive, what if we outgrow the space before then?"

"Now you're talking," said Fred, enjoying the discussion and Judy's enthusiasm. "I hope that's prophetic."

"How about the place out on Myrtle Avenue?" asked Judy. "It's really nice."

"Yeah, but I think it's too far off the beaten path. Not sure people are willing to go much out of their way just for cupcakes, even great ones like yours."

Judy's cupcakes were legendary. There were several kinds from old family recipes she'd tweaked to fit modern tastes. They were a sure fire hit at the church covered dish suppers, especially among the children, and her neighbors and her five grandchildren were always grateful for a supply. What better idea for a business than to sell "Judy's Own Old Time Recipe" cupcakes? They hadn't decided on a name for the store yet, but Fred had some ideas.

"Then I guess that leaves the one in the strip center on Wellover Street," said Judy. "Good traffic, good parking, easy in and out, the other stores there are nice, and it really has the layout we need."

"That one's kind of been my favorite too, even though the rent will be higher. You wanna do it?"

"Let's. You can talk to the agent tomorrow. More pizza?"

A month earlier, Fred and Judy had sat in their living room one evening with Judy's brother, Bill, an accountant, and Jack, one of Fred's golfing buddies who'd recently retired from running a small florist shop after selling it to his son. Fred had opened the meeting with prayer and then spoke to the group.

"Thanks for coming. And since I know you're not all Christians here, thanks for letting me pray. Judy and I think it's pretty important.

"We've been talking for some time about this business idea Judy and I have, and tonight I wanted to show you an outline of the plan we've worked up. I'm just an old machinist who doesn't know much about how to run a business, but you guys do and I think we could really use your input before we invest our life savings. I know the product's good because people rave about Judy's cupcakes, and lately she's been testing new recipes on neighbors, and strangers too, to make sure people aren't just being polite when they say they like them. It's the rest of it we're not so sure about."

The meeting was long, and they discussed matters that left Fred's head spinning, but with Judy's encouragement he revised the business plan using many of the suggestions they'd been given.

Two suggestions in particular were especially challenging. Bill had said, "The first thing I tell anyone starting up a new business is, 'Budget twice as much money and twice as much time as you really think you'll need before you turn a profit.' New business owners are always too optimistic and unrealistic."

"And I would also say, choose your team wisely," offered Jack.

"But," Fred protested, "the team is just me and Judy, right?"

"You'll find it's bigger than that, especially once you start hiring, and also when you start picking trusted suppliers," Jack said. "And even though we won't be involved on a day-to-day basis, Bill and I are on sort of an extended team with you if you want us to be. Right, Bill?"

Bill nodded his enthusiastic assent.

"Of course, we want you to be," said Judy.

"You should read this book I have, called *The Five-fold Effect*," said Jack. "It has leadership and management concepts based on Ephesians 4:11–16. I wish I'd read it when I was running the florist shop. I'll lend you my copy."[93]

Fred and Judy ran the revised plan by Bill and Jack, and they prayed over it until they felt a peace about it. In the next weeks they started lining things up to open the store.

Fred wanted to call it CupKake City. "Kind of cute with the 'K,' don't you think?" he'd said. "Won't the ladies like that?"

The advertising agency had convinced him otherwise, to Judy's immense relief. "It's clever but a little too cute, and anyway women aren't your only customers," they'd pointed out diplomatically. Their recommendation, The Cup & Cake, resonated well with everybody Fred and Judy tried it out on, so Fred accepted it gracefully. They were taking a suggestion of Bill's to offer coffee along with the cupcakes, so it was a fitting name.

As soon as Fred and Judy signed the lease on the store, and before they started cleaning and setting it up, they went inside and prayed over it, dedicating the business to God and asking for His wisdom, favor and protection. They walked the parking lot and the alley behind the strip center praying for all the other businesses to be blessed, as well as their landlord, their employees, customers, suppliers, tradesmen, and anyone else who might come on the property.

The Cup & Cake opened on schedule. It had taken a lot of hard work to get everything ready, but Fred was elated. The kitchen was

---

93   Of course, Jack should have bought them a new copy!

spotless. The fixtures and equipment gleamed. Everything worked flawlessly. "The floor is so clean you could eat off it!" he declared.

Grand Opening week was a rousing success, cupcakes flying off the shelves. Customers came and went at a furious pace, many commenting on how nice the store looked and how clean it was. Judy had done a good job of decorating when she wasn't toiling over the ovens, although to Fred's eye it seemed like a lot of frou-frou. But he was proud of her efforts, and he told her so. He could see the customers liked it.

Their daughter, Kate, called on opening day with her congratulations. "I love the Website, Mom and Dad," she added. "And I made sure to 'Like' you on Facebook. Sorry I live so far away or I'd be your best customer."

For the next several weeks business was brisk as more and more people tried the new cupcake store, which was sort of a novelty in town. The ad agency had come highly recommended by Jack, and they had planned the launch well. There were radio and TV spots and ads and flyers with coupons in the paper. The Cup & Cake got good reviews in the "Weekender" section of the paper, and Judy was interviewed on the morning show at the TV station. After the initial push, there was still enough money in the ad budget to run a low level reminder campaign for at least the next 12 months. Some customers said they hadn't seen the ads but came because their friends had told them the cupcakes and coffee were really good. The Cup & Cake was off to a great start.

Making sure the cupcakes were good was the highest priority. Judy set the menu and handled all the ordering of ingredients to ensure quality, with Fred stepping in only if necessary to handle any suppliers who seemed to be giving Judy a hard time. "You're building a brand here," the ad agency people said. "Consistency is critical. People need to know they can get the same thing this week that they got last week. Otherwise, what does the brand stand for?" Fred knew they were right. He'd seen the same thing when ordering parts for machines at the plant, so he and Judy passed up some attractive deals on substitute ingredients.

One evening as they were cleaning up after closing, Julius, the college student who worked the cash register part time, had an idea. "There's room for three or four tables and chairs. Why not let people sit here and eat their cupcakes with their coffee instead of having only take-out?"

Judy thought it was a great plan.

Fred dope-slapped his forehead. "Why didn't I think of that?" he said. "We'll have to hire somebody to serve tables, but employing more people is a good thing too, isn't it, especially if business picks up? Hey, Julius, how'd you like to work full time?"

"Love to, but I'm spending next semester in Paris."

"Too bad for us," said Fred. "The customers really like you, I've noticed. Some of them even call you by name, and you know a lot of them too. You're a great evangelist for the Cup & Cake, as we thought you would be when we hired you. We'll miss you."

"Well, I do have some friends who might be interested in working here," Julius offered.

"Be sure and bring back some cupcake recipes from France!" said Judy.

"Can I tell you something else?" asked Julius.

"You're on a roll here. Shoot."

"Well, lately a few of the customers have been saying they'd like to buy the cupcakes in the supermarket. They like coming here, but it would be more convenient sometimes."

"Really?" said Fred. "I seem to remember Bill or Jack talking about that a few months ago, and I just didn't see how it would make any sense. But if people are asking for them, maybe…"

"I think they call it 'market segmentation,'" said Julius. "I've been taking business courses."

Later at home, Fred and Judy discussed the idea. It would mean buying new equipment to increase capacity and hiring somebody to help Judy with the baking. Maybe hiring a salesperson too. There would be package design and labeling issues, and they'd probably need to buy a truck to make the deliveries. But they did have room for expansion, and with orders from a supermarket chain in hand they might be able to borrow the money needed. "Let's see what Bill and Jack think about it," Fred suggested. Bill and Jack thought it was a realistic goal and made some suggestions. Fred and Judy decided to put a rough plan together. Two weeks later Fred called Harris Teeter and Food Lion to set up appointments to explore the idea.

Six months went by while the business thrived and grew. The tables were usually full, and a cadre of regulars had formed. The free Wi-Fi had helped too, along with the attractive Website that let people look at the menu, order ahead and pick up their orders when they arrived instead of having to wait (Julius's ideas again).

They had gotten a contract with Harris Teeter. The chain's buyer and the ad agency were working with Judy on packaging. New ovens had arrived and were being tested while Judy trained a new baker she had recruited away from a restaurant across town. The bank loan had come with an offer of business advice, which Fred was happy to listen to. The increasingly complex bookkeeping had been turned over to Bill's accounting firm, with Fred and Judy carefully reviewing the numbers every week. They presented a summary of this to everyone in their regular weekly employee meetings.

At the meetings, everyone was invited to bring up any issues or suggestions that were on their minds (or they could see Fred or Judy privately any time if they preferred). Some interesting ideas often came out of the discussions, and occasional problems Fred and Judy were unaware of were highlighted before they could fester.

The Cup & Cake was putting money in the bank even after paying the loan interest. Fred was beginning to see what the business could possibly look like in five or ten years. It was hard work, with long hours, but things were looking very good.

Then the unthinkable happened. Fred got sick.

"It's his heart," the doctor said. "He won't be able to go to work for eight weeks, and even after that he won't be able to keep up the same pace. He should think about retiring."

"He's definitely not ready for that," Judy said.

"Well then, I guess if he's doing something he really loves, it will be healthy enough."

Fortunately, Judy was able to step into Fred's shoes and run the business while he was on the mend. It wasn't easy, but since they had worked closely together on every aspect of it except the actual baking, she knew what was where and what needed to be done. She "rallied the troops" around her and they closed ranks to help out as much as they could, putting in extra effort until Fred was ready to come back. Jack dropped in from time to time for coffee with Judy, allowing her to vent about various issues that came up and offering moral support along with practical suggestions from his own business experience. Daughter Kate flew in to help out, staying as long as she could before going back home to her husband and two toddlers. At Judy's request, church friends prayed for Fred's recovery, for protection of the business, and for Judy and the employees. Insurance covered most of Fred's medical expenses, and income from The Cup & Cake covered the rest, including three weeks of home nursing service until Fred could take care of himself.

Fred came back fully recovered, although he was on a strict exercise and diet regimen that allowed him only a fraction of the cupcakes he'd been eating before. That made him a little grumpy at first, but he got used to it. He was especially gratified that the Cup & Cake's restaurant sanitation rating of 101.5 hadn't slipped a bit.

Everybody who pitched in to help while he was away got bonuses as a thank you.

Julius, back from Paris, graduated from college with a business degree, and Fred and Judy hired him to be the assistant store manager, freeing Fred to work on a plan to open a second location. After Julius got settled in, Fred and Judy took a two week vacation, the first they'd had in several years.

Today, The Cup & Cake is a robust multimillion dollar enterprise with 14 locations in three states, over 400 employees, wide supermarket distribution, an Internet mail order operation, a coffee break catering service for businesses, and a cooking school.

"It's all about good maintenance and planning ahead," Fred says quite often, "and praise God for really good advisors too. Just look and see how our Cup & Cake runneth over!"

Discussion

This version has a completely different feeling about it, doesn't it? Why? It's because The Cup & Cake experienced The Five-fold Effect!

First, the whole enterprise was bathed in prayer even when it was still just an idea in Fred's and Judy's minds. Then, they kept God involved every step of the way.

Second, we know from his pre-retirement background that this Fred already had an appreciation for the value of teamwork. So this time there was a real team, not just Fred and a bunch of helpers. Fred had strong ideas, and his ego tried to poke through a few times, but he always carefully considered the counsel of the team members before arriving at big decisions, usually by consensus. The team actually had three levels: the official or legal leadership team of Fred and Judy; the immediate team of Fred, Judy and the employees; and the extended team that included Bill and Jack as sort of unofficial board members, plus the ad agency and others. All of these provided five-fold input. Early on, there was a team even before there was a final plan, Fred's and Judy's version of getting the right people on the bus before driving it away.

Third, he and Judy counted the cost before risking their life savings on the venture. They not only had a budget first, but also a well thought out strategic plan and a realistic timetable, with money in reserve. They didn't know how to come up with such a plan on their own, so they sought help from people who did.

They treated the plan as a "living" document, not a static recipe or formula, and they tweaked it along the way as problems or new opportunities arose, again seeking and carefully considering input from all appropriate sources. As a result, all the team members felt like they had a stake in the success or failure of the enterprise, not just Fred and Judy, so when Fred got sick and the crunch came, they all willingly pitched in to help, having been equipped ahead of time through Fred's openness and willingness to involve them in all aspects of the business. He didn't carry all the burdens himself.

"Well then, how come he got sick anyway?" you may ask.

I don't know. It happens. Maybe the enemy just didn't like him having all that success. The important thing is, when it happened the team was prepared, unlike in the first story, and the business survived and went on to flourish.

While they may not have done it religiously, Fred and Judy apparently did intentionally look around and ask, "Who is my prophetic person, who is our evangelist...?" and so on, or at least they seemed to have that idea in mind, so we can assume they did read Ephesians 4:11–16 and the book you're reading now. Their results reflected this, as will yours!

So just who were their five-fold people? Fred, of course, was the apostolic one, dedicated to the business, providing the vision (after weighing input from others on the team), and setting the tone or atmosphere in which the rest of the team felt loved, respected and needed and understood where they fit on the team. He was a good father figure, providing for the business, giving identity to the team members, and being prepared to protect them if necessary, as with Judy when she encountered discourteous suppliers. (It would have been the same if Judy had been in charge instead of Fred. Apostolic behavior is not tied to gender.)

Fred himself identified Judy as prophetic. It is not unusual, by the way, for husband and wife teams to be gifted as apostolic and prophetic, respectively. I believe God often plans it that way. Both Bill and Jack had prophetic input with several suggestions, including the idea of selling through supermarkets, even though Fred didn't pick up on it until Julius reported what some of the customers were saying. The ad agency provided sound advice on marketing strategy and brand building.

Fred and Judy called Julius evangelistic, and he was. It doesn't say in the story, but Julius probably talked up the Cup & Cake at the college, handing out coupons and drumming up new business. The ad agency people did their evangelistic job well too. Although Julius didn't have an apostolic role through most of the story, he did demonstrate those traits through his persistent interest in the well-being of the enterprise and his choice to take business courses at the college. It is likely Fred mentored him as he assumed the apostolic role of assistant manager upon graduation.

It looks like Fred (and Judy too) was a good teacher, showing the employees how to sell, take care of the equipment and keep the place clean. Bill probably taught Fred about how to set up and keep the books at first, and Fred probably taught Judy about how to order supplies and ingredients. Judy taught her recipes to the new baker. Julius probably proved to be a good teacher in his role as assistant manager.

What about pastoral? Judy encouraged Fred as he dealt with the realization he still had a lot to learn and more work to do based on the advice Bill and Jack gave him at their initial meeting. No doubt she was nurturing and encouraging to Fred when he was sick, and she probably had to reassure the employees too that everything would be all right. Jack and Kate also provided pastoral support for both Fred and Judy during that stressful time. Even the doctor, though not really on the team from the beginning, had an encouraging attitude, as opposed to the first doctor who essentially declared a death sentence over Fred with his prognosis.

"Okay," you may be saying, "I see how everybody pitched in with their various five-fold gifts, and I understand that's to be expected because God often doesn't endow each person with only one, but shouldn't we see a predominant gift, or two at the most, in each person?" Yes, we should. Here's how I would say that looks for the story's main characters (Table 16–1). See if you agree.

Table 16-1: Predominant and Secondary Five-Fold Gifts Seen in the Main Characters

Character	Five-Fold Gifts in Operation Predominant (Secondary)
Fred	Apostolic, (Teaching)
Judy	Prophetic, Pastoral, (Teaching)
Julius	Evangelistic, Apostolic, (Teaching)
Bill	Prophetic
Jack	Prophetic, (Pastoral)
Ad Agency	Evangelistic
Kate	Pastoral

There is another key point to be made here. As you can see, at various times in the story, some of the characters performed various roles in the five-fold mix that were outside their predominant giftings. For example, Judy had three roles that are easy to identify, of which I would say teaching was a secondary one. Each of us is capable, by the power of the Holy Spirit, to occupy any of the five roles when it's called for by a specific situation or need, or for a season. You may occupy several roles simultaneously. You should ask, "Who do I need to be for this situation?" And, "Who does (so and so) need to be for me in this situation?" Remember too, you may have one set of roles for a season and another for another season.

Let's see how this looks when we put it into our familiar schematic (Figure 16–1).

**Figure 16–1: Distribution of Five-Fold Gifts
among the Main Characters**

As you read the next chapter (Chapter 17 – What Does it Look Like When it Works?), think back to this one and see how many of The Five-fold Effect success factors are evident in the story of The Cup & Cake. I hope this story has inspired you to seriously consider applying five-fold to your situation.

ACTIVATION EXERCISES

1. See if you agree with my assessment of the five-fold gifts of the main characters, from the chart. If not, how would you change it?

2. What advice would you offer Fred and Judy about how they could have done things even better?

3. Are you hungry for a good cupcake right now?

CHAPTER 17

WHAT DOES IT LOOK LIKE WHEN IT WORKS?

THE "VALUE PROPOSITION"

How do you measure success? I mean, how do *you* measure success? The measures will be different for every organization. Most businesses measure it primarily in terms of sales and profits. Departments within companies might measure it in terms of staff size and budget growth (although this can lead to counter-productive "empire building"). A committee or task force might say what's important is that they did a good job on time and within budget. All of those criteria, and any others that may apply to whatever your organization is up to, can be considered "fruit." And of course, the key is to "look at the fruit." Don't look just at sales, staffing, budgets, seats filled, attendance, and so on, without relating all that to the *purpose* of the enterprise. *Is the organization fulfilling its purpose well?*

And how apparent are the effects of successful employment of five-fold or apostolic leadership? What does "The Five-fold Effect" look like?

What does it look like when we have a leadership team representing each of the five-fold gifts, under the authority of a leader with apostolic gifting, determining what is the work that should be done and equipping the members of the organization to do it? How can we tell if we are seeing "The whole body, joined and knit together...by which every part does its share... causing growth of the body," a fully functioning, well coordinated organization, every member of which is perfectly placed and equipped to do, and is doing, a needed job that perfectly contributes to the success of the enterprise?

This is what some might refer to as the "value proposition," or the compelling reasons for employing the five-fold paradigm. In addition to seeing favorable answers to the checklist of questions for the accountability group from Chapter 13, there will be some very telling signs that things are working well.

You Can Tell By:

1. The way the leaders work together, honoring each other's gifts and talents

2. The way the leaders ensure that their people see and share the vision for the enterprise and work to train and prepare them for roles that are a good fit between the needs of the organization and the people's talents (gifts), skills and interests (equipping, from Ephesians 4:11–12a)

3. How the group works with excellence and integrity, "as unto the Lord" (Colossians 3:23–24: "Whatever you do, work at it with all your heart, as working for the Lord, not for men, since you know that you will receive an inheritance from the Lord as a reward. It is the Lord Christ you are serving.")

4. The love, honor and friendship the group has for one another (John 13:34: "A new command I give you: Love one another. As I have loved you, so you must love one another. By this all men will know that you are my disciples, if you love one another.")

5. The compassion, concern, and preference the group shows one another (Philippians 2: 3–4: "Do nothing out of selfish ambition or vain conceit, but in humility consider others better than yourselves. Each of you should look not only to your own interests, but also to the interests of others.")

6. Wise, God-honoring decisions that recognize God's plan for and sovereignty over the marketplace (Proverbs 1:7: "The fear of the Lord is the beginning of knowledge, but fools despise wisdom and discipline." Psalms 24:1: "The earth is the Lord's, and everything in it, the world, and all who live in it.")

7. The resulting unity and alignment of purpose, fostering peace and harmony in the group (Romans 15:2, 5–6: "Each of us should please his neighbor for his good, to build him up. May the God who gives endurance and encouragement give you a spirit of unity among yourselves as you follow Christ Jesus, so that with one heart and mouth you may glorify the God and Father of our Lord Jesus Christ." Ephesians 4:12–13: "to prepare God's people for works of service, so that the body of Christ may be built up until we all reach unity in the faith and in the knowledge of the Son of God and become mature, attaining to the whole measure of the fullness of Christ.")

8. A balance of focus and functional emphasis appropriate to the mission

9. God's favor on the group (Deuteronomy 8:18: "But remember the Lord your God, for it is he who gives you

the ability to produce wealth, and so confirms his covenant, which he swore to your forefathers, as it is today." Proverbs 22:29: "Do you see a man skilled in his work? He will serve before kings; he will not serve before obscure men.")

10. The application of judicious pruning. Admonition and correction are delivered lovingly; people are reassigned, given more training or promoted as they grow and/or as needs change. Pruning is considered not as punishment but as the reward for growth (John 15:2).

11. God is glorified by the transformed group and its results or product (1 Peter 2:12: "having your conduct honorable among the Gentiles, that when they speak against you as evildoers, they may, by your good works which they observe, glorify God in the day of visitation" (NKJV). Matthew 5:16: "In the same way, let your light shine before men, that they may see your good deeds and praise your Father in heaven.")

Didn't we see most if not all of these characteristics in play at The Cup & Cake? Notice, too, how well this list lines up with the fruit of the Spirit: love, joy, peace, longsuffering, kindness, goodness, faithfulness, gentleness, and self-control (Galatians 5:22–23). Look for parallels in all organizations that apply the five-fold leadership principles.

And look for greater success. *God's principles work. What a powerful tool this knowledge will be in the hands of you the believer in the marketplace! And what a powerful testimony to the glory of God will be its effective application.*

Recall Zechariah's vision from Chapter 3, a beautiful picture of what the "city" looks like when it's working properly according to God's plan. It's a picture of the Eden God always intended when he charged Adam and Eve to take dominion over the earth! It is the church inseparable from society, in which God lives by His Spirit, protecting His people with flames of holy fire. As we take dominion over the seven mountains of influence in the name of Jesus, the world moves closer to being restored from its separation from God. And He gets all the glory.

Again, in the words of Paul in Ephesians 2:19–22 (italics added):

"Consequently, you are no longer foreigners and aliens, but fellow citizens with God's people and members of God's household, built on the foundation of the *apostles and prophets*, with Christ Jesus himself as the chief cornerstone. In him the whole building is joined together and rises to become a holy temple in the Lord. And in him you too are being built together to become a dwelling in which God lives by his Spirit."

DO YOU THINK THIS IS A GOOD BOOK?

We're getting close to the end of the book. If you do think this book is well done and will be useful to you, I want you to know that I learned most of what's in it, and how to put it together in a book, by reading and listening to the teachings of, and talking with, many gifted apostolic, prophetic, evangelistic, teaching and pastoral people whose ministries have touched my life and encouraged and equipped me for this work. They are too many to list, although I have mentioned several of them. I thank the Holy Spirit for the initial and continuing vision for the book, and I give glory to God for whatever good comes of it.

CHAPTER 18

PREPARE YOURSELF – THE REAL STARTING POINT

"Wait a minute," I hear someone saying, "We've covered a lot of ground, and there are many new ideas in this book, and now you say we're still at the starting point!" That's right. We have covered a lot, but we're still not quite ready. Even before stepping into the practical aspects of applying five-fold leadership principles in our lives, we need to take a step back for a wider look at this new paradigm and ask how we should prepare ourselves to think about it.

I hope you are excited. I hope you are not overwhelmed. There is no need to be. Just take things one step at a time, asking the Holy Spirit for help. He will give it. That's who He is.

The starting point I have in mind is the one I first called to your attention in the Introduction and again in Chapter 13. It is Romans 12. I hope you've read it already. If not, it's still in Appendix A. Read and meditate on it. In it you will find instructions essential to adopting the heart and mind attitude we all need to have in order to be prepared to serve God and each other in any way, including by the application of five-fold leadership. It is an excellent expansion on the practice of other-centered love.

Understand that meditating means absorbing more than just head knowledge of the words on the page. Believe that as you look deeply into God's Word He will show you truths that will come alive not only in your mind but also in your spirit. The Word is life, and life produces life. The Word will be a blessing to you and to others who benefit from your understanding as you apply it. God's Word carries transforming power, for when we see God as He is revealed in it, then we will become more like Him as we walk out what we see. It also carries a prophetic property in that what we see we can have. That is why vision is so important, as are the stories of others who have seen or experienced what we are seeking.

ACTIVATION EXERCISES

1. Read Romans 12. Take the time to meditate on it. Ask the Holy Spirit to show you things in it that maybe you've never seen, understood, or knew how to apply before.

2. Ask God to show you any areas from Romans 12 that you could do better in. List them and pray and ask God to help you with them. He doesn't see them as weaknesses but rather areas where you haven't yet experienced Him enough. He wants to promote and strengthen you in them because He already sees you as whole, complete, and walking in your destiny.

3. Make Your Plan: Ask yourself if you seriously want to become a five-fold leader and use the principles in this book to help lead your business or organization to greater success. If the answer is "yes," start now by preparing a personal game plan to begin applying what you've learned here. List the steps in your plan and how you would carry them out. Resolve to begin taking the steps, and then do so.

Ready?

Okay, finally, at last, *now* go and begin to experience The Five-fold Effect!

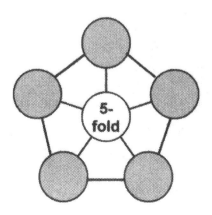

APPENDIX A

Romans 12

1 Therefore, I urge you, brothers, in view of God's mercy, to offer your bodies as living sacrifices, holy and pleasing to God—this is your spiritual act of worship. 2 Do not conform any longer to the pattern of this world, but be transformed by the renewing of your mind. Then you will be able to test and approve what God's will is—his good, pleasing and perfect will.

3 For by the grace given me I say to every one of you: Do not think of yourself more highly than you ought, but rather think of yourself with sober judgment, in accordance with the measure of faith God has given you. 4 Just as each of us has one body with many members, and these members do not all have the same function, 5 so in Christ we who are many form one body, and each member belongs to all the others. 6 We have different gifts, according to the grace given us. If a man's gift is prophesying, let him use it in proportion to his faith. 7 If it is serving, let him serve; if it is teaching, let him teach; 8 if it is encouraging, let him encourage; if it is contributing to the needs of others, let him give generously; if it is leadership, let him govern diligently; if it is showing mercy, let him do it cheerfully.

9 Love must be sincere. Hate what is evil; cling to what is good. 10 Be devoted to one another in brotherly love. Honor one another above yourselves. 11 Never be lacking in zeal, but keep

your spiritual fervor, serving the Lord. 12 Be joyful in hope, patient in affliction, faithful in prayer. 13 Share with God's people who are in need. Practice hospitality.

14 Bless those who persecute you; bless and do not curse. 15 Rejoice with those who rejoice; mourn with those who mourn. 16 Live in harmony with one another. Do not be proud, but be willing to associate with people of low position. Do not be conceited.

17 Do not repay anyone evil for evil. Be careful to do what is right in the eyes of everybody. 18 If it is possible, as far as it depends on you, live at peace with everyone. 19 Do not take revenge, my friends, but leave room for God's wrath, for it is written: "It is mine to avenge; I will repay," says the Lord. 20 On the contrary:

"If your enemy is hungry, feed him;
if he is thirsty, give him something to drink.
In doing this, you will heap burning coals on his head."

21 Do not be overcome by evil, but overcome evil with good.

The Holy Bible: New International Version

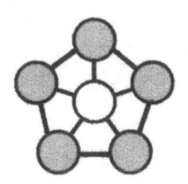

APPENDIX B

A Daily Apostolic Prayer

Lord, I acknowledge and thank You that all authority comes from You. I thank you for those in authority over me, and I ask You to bless them, in Jesus' name. Thank you for this assignment You have given me for or concerning (organization, endeavor, task, responsibility, etc.). Now I ask You to help me with it.

Right now I claim the promise of 2 Chronicles 7:14, bowing before You, seeking Your face and asking You to show me any ways from which I need to repent. (Pause and listen) I do repent of _____ and ask for Your forgiveness and for Your healing touch upon me, upon those I work with, and upon the endeavor You have called me to.

Lord, please bless (organization or endeavor) and bring a spirit of unity to it. Show me who I need to be for everyone involved, and show them, and me, who they need to be for me. Thank You for showing me who has the gift of prophecy or discernment, who has the gift of pastoring or compassion, the gift of teaching, the gift of evangelism or persuasion, and the gifts of administration and serving and any other gifts according to how these gifts are needed to carry out the work You have planned for this endeavor. Thank You for showing me how to help each of these people to walk out the destiny You have for them. I pray for wisdom, vision, revelation, plans, provision, courage and perseverance.

Thank You for showing us how to work together in unity

according to Ephesians 4:11–16 so that the whole organization grows and builds itself up in love as each part does its work according to Your purposes.

Thank you for the success You have promised with this assignment. I give You all the glory for it.

In Jesus' name I pray. Amen.

2 Chronicles 7:14: "If my people, who are called by my name, will humble themselves and pray and seek my face and turn from their wicked ways, then will I hear from heaven and will forgive their sin and will heal their land."

Ephesians 4:11–16: "It was he who gave some to be apostles, some to be prophets, some to be evangelists, and some to be pastors and teachers, to prepare God's people for works of service, so that the body of Christ may be built up until we all reach unity in the faith and in the knowledge of the Son of God and become mature, attaining to the whole measure of the fullness of Christ. Then we will no longer be infants, tossed back and forth by the waves, and blown here and there by every wind of teaching and by the cunning and craftiness of men in their deceitful scheming. Instead, speaking the truth in love, we will in all things grow up into him who is the Head, that is, Christ. From him the whole body, joined and held together by every supporting ligament, grows and builds itself up in love, as each part does its work."

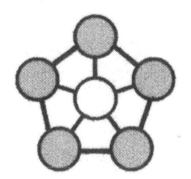

APPENDIX C

Impartation of Spiritual Gifts

Like any spiritual gift (but not an office—see below), if you have it you can pray for it to be imparted to others by the power of the Holy Spirit. If you want such a gift, or want more of it, you can ask for an impartation prayer from someone who has it.

International healing evangelist, speaker and author Randy Clark is all about the impartation of his gifts for evangelism, for pastoring and for healing the sick. At his Global Awakening conferences and schools of healing, and on ministry trips to Brazil and other nations, he schedules multiple impartation services for the ministry teams, the pastors in attendance, and the congregants. At many services, the ministry team members under Randy's apostolic authority also pray for impartation of gifts to pastors and congregants, so it isn't only Randy doing it by himself. This is an important exercise of the mandate to "equip the saints."

When Randy prays for impartation of his healing or other gifts to others, a number of things may happen:

1. Some people may receive the gift being prayed for, e.g., the gift of healing (being able to heal others), who did not have it before.

2. Some who had the gift but did not know it may become aware of it and begin to exercise the gift, healing the sick. It didn't need to be imparted, only ignited.

3. Some who have been operating in the gift will find it becoming stronger as manifested in a greater desire to heal the sick and greater effectiveness when they try to do so.

4. Some will find their gift surpasses even Randy's.

5. For some, there may be no outward manifestation of impartation. But since we know Jesus commanded *all* of us to heal the sick, we know that some capacity to do so resides within each of us, with or without a prayer of impartation from anyone. There may be factors that block the manifestation, such as inner healing issues, unforgiveness, fear, and so on, that need to be dealt with before the person can operate effectively in this gift.

6. In a relatively few instances, some may receive a commissioning to operate in the gifts to a magnified degree, even to the extent of a sovereign calling to an office, as in the cases of Heidi Baker, Leif Hetland and Henry Madava, for example (See "Greater Works," below.).

Let me say a few words more about #4 above. Some people say, "I can't impart what I don't have." That may be strictly true, but I do not see it as a limitation. In the first place, it's not you (or Randy Clark, as he makes clear below) who is imparting. It is God imparting through you. And God's supply of whatever is being imparted is limitless.

In the Old Testament, impartations were directly from God. The first instance of this is recorded in Numbers 11:16–17 where God takes some of the Spirit he had given to Moses and puts it on the 70 elders.

"The Lord said to Moses: 'Bring me seventy of Israel's elders who are known to you as leaders and officials among the people. Have them come to the Tent of Meeting, that they may stand there with you. I will come down and speak with you there, and I will take of the Spirit that is on you and put the Spirit on them. They will help you carry the burden of the people so that you will not have to carry it alone.'"

There is no evidence that Moses was in any way diminished by this. He still had the same Spirit on him. There is an endless supply of Holy Spirit.

When Elisha got a double portion of what Elijah had, he didn't get it from Elijah. He got it from God (2 Kings 2:14–15). In Hebrews 6:2 we learn about the laying on of hands for impartation and other purposes as God now works through us to accomplish things he usually did directly in the Old Testament.

Two conclusions follow from this: (A) You can receive an impartation greater than that of the person praying for you, and (B) therefore, although I think it is better to ask for an impartation from someone who has the gift you want more of, I do believe you can receive an impartation for something the person praying doesn't even have!

One reason I think it is better to receive from someone who already has the gift you are seeking, or seeking more of, is that the spirit of that gift is already present, and it can actually "leak" from that person to you, often without either one of you praying. Another reason is that there is an opportunity to learn from that person, giving you a head start when the impartation does come. The principle is the same as "If you want to be a carpenter, hang around with carpenters." See what they do. Do what they do. Yes, it may take practice, but much of what they do will rub off on you if you have the desire, or at the very least you will learn more and learn faster. By the same token, if you want to learn how to heal, or prophesy, or teach, or whatever it is, keep the company of those who already do it more than you.

GREATER WORKS

Jesus said, "Greater works than these will you do" (John 14:12), and that applies to impartation. "Greater works than Randy Clark's will you do," has been true for many people. Among the most notable are Heidi Baker who, with her husband, Rolland, have planted over 10,000 churches in Mozambique and seen over one million people come to the Lord and over 450 raised from the dead; Leif Hetland who has seen at least one million people become believers in 76 nations, including places that were totally closed to the Gospel; and Henry Madava of Ukraine who also has seen one million salvations through his ministry. All received impartations from Randy Clark before these events took place, but theirs are not works of Randy Clark even though God used him in an important way.[94]

Randy makes it clear that he takes no credit for the work the Holy Spirit does through him. As he puts it, to some people "this seems almost like I can cause an impartation to come upon anyone for a gift though not an office. I am not sure it actually works that way. It seems to me, that as the word is taught and testimonies are given, faith is created, causing an atmosphere more conducive to receiving. However, it is also a sovereign issue. All are strengthened by the Spirit, some receive a gifting or anointing, and a relatively few in comparison receive a commissioning like Heidi, Leif, or Henry. This is definitely a God thing, and I don't really have any control over who gets what. Though used in the impartation, it is much more like Balaam's ass[95] than anything I can take credit for."[96]

---

94   It is important to point out that Global Awakening (the ministry founded by Randy Clark) and The Toronto Airport Christian Fellowship (pastored by John and Carol Arnott and where the Holy Spirit used Randy and others for many impartations, including Heidi Baker's) are five-fold ministries. Their impact has been supernaturally effective as seen in the statistics above and thousands more untold stories like these, far, far beyond the growth in budget and staff of either of these organizations. Again, these are not marketplace examples, *per se*, but they do impact the marketplace, and they are forerunners to what can happen when five-fold is intentionally applied in other organizations, including yours.

95   Numbers 22:21–38

96   E-mail correspondence, April 2, 2012

Equally important to note is that none of these people, nor anyone else, has become another Randy Clark. The Holy Spirit works differently in each of us, and so when we are tempted to say to someone whose spiritual gifts we admire, "I want to walk in your gifting" (sometimes called "anointing"), we should refrain. That's like saying, "I want to ride your bicycle." What you should say is, "I want to ride my own bicycle, but I want to be able to ride it as well as you ride yours." In other words, "I want to walk in my own gifting but with a measure of it that is more like how well you walk in yours."

Because God gave it to you, your own gifting or anointing fits you perfectly and accomplishes what God has for you if you will let it. Because it is from God it is powerful. You should never have the attitude that God has given you something inferior. Embrace your uniqueness as you see yourself through God's eyes.

By the same token, don't fail to walk in power because of a fear that you will become proud. God says just to start walking and He will adjust your attitude. You will learn to be proud of your God!

As for contending that you can receive an impartation of something the person praying doesn't have, I am also relying on the Scripture that says, "Again, I tell you that if two of you on earth agree about anything you ask for, it will be done for you by my Father in heaven" (Matthew 18:19).[97]

WHAT ABOUT GIFTS BESIDES HEALING AND THE FIVE-FOLD GIFTS?

I didn't think about the impartation of other gifts until I was on a ministry trip in Brazil and became acquainted with a man and his wife from the Midwest who were on our team. He was retiring from a secular career and planning to take on an administrative role

---

97   Also see Matthew 21:22; Mark 11:24; Luke 11:9; John 14:13, 15:7, 15:16, and 16:23.

at the church where his son was pastor. "But he's not administrative at all," opined his wife, with genuine concern that I could see he shared as well. I do have administrative ability, and before I knew what was happening I heard myself asking, "Would you like me to pray a prayer of impartation of my administrative gifts to you?" He enthusiastically took me up on it, and I could sense his faith and confidence rising.

Six years later I ran into him and his wife again at a conference. While I can't claim he had become an administrative giant, he told me things were going well in his new role, so I believe it helped. Upon request, I have prayed this impartation for a few other people since first praying it for him.

On the other end of the spectrum is my wife, Carol, who has many wonderful gifts, including those of an artist and an intercessor, and she is very comfortable in her right braininess. Carol is not administratively gifted and does not want to be. She is content to rely on me for family administrative stuff. On occasion, I have threatened to wait until she is asleep some night and secretly pray a prayer of impartation over her for the gift of administration. She doesn't like that, but so far she hasn't taken to wearing a necklace of garlic cloves to bed. I suppose if it's against her will it wouldn't work anyway.

I have had singers and musicians pray prayers of impartation over me for improvement in my vocal ability and skill at guitar playing, at which I am a novice, having started it relatively late in life instead of in my teens like most good players. I have seen improvement as I've practiced and hung around other guitar players, and I attribute much of it to those prayers. However, the reason I'm writing a book instead of appearing at Carnegie Hall in the footsteps of Andrés Segovia is that I am called to be a writer, among other things, but not a musician. And yes, I do know how to get to Carnegie Hall, as the old story goes: Practice, practice, practice! Or in my case, use the GPS.

CAN THE FIVE-FOLD OFFICES BE IMPARTED?

You might ask, "Can the five-fold offices be imparted by one person to another like the gift of healing or of administration, or communication skills, or musical ability?" No, the *offices* of apostle, prophet, and so on, cannot be imparted, but the gifts associated with them can be, as can all gifts and talents endowed by God. The office itself is a calling and an ordination from God and cannot be conferred except by Him, although such a commissioning sometimes may happen sovereignly during an impartation prayer as we saw above.

But what about Elijah and Elisha?

So Elijah went from there and found Elisha son of Shaphat. He was plowing with twelve yoke of oxen, and he himself was driving the twelfth pair. Elijah went up to him and *threw his cloak around him* (1 Kings 19:19, italics added).

When they had crossed, Elijah said to Elisha, "Tell me, what can I do for you before I am taken from you?" *"Let me inherit a double portion of your spirit," Elisha replied.* "You have asked a difficult thing," Elijah said, "yet *if you see me when I am taken from you, it will be yours*—otherwise not" (2 Kings 2:9–10, italics added).

Then he took the cloak that had fallen from him and struck the water with it. "Where now is the Lord, the God of Elijah?" he asked. When he struck the water, it divided to the right and to the left, and he crossed over. The company of the prophets from Jericho, who were watching, said, *"The spirit of Elijah is resting on Elisha."* And they went to meet him and bowed to the ground before him (2 Kings 2:14–15, italics added).

When Elijah cast his cloak (or mantle) upon Elisha, it was not an impartation but rather a prophetic public statement of what the Lord had already decreed for Elisha, that he was anointed as a prophet and would succeed Elijah in the office. When Elisha picked up Elijah's mantle after Elijah was taken up into Heaven, it was his prophetic act of stepping into his promotion to Elijah's office and the additional supernatural power that accompanied it. It may have been an impartation of additional prophetic gifting and skill, and no doubt during his lifetime Elijah imparted measures of such skill to Elijah from time to time, but Elisha was already a prophet by the calling of God. Even when Elijah said Elisha would get a double portion if he saw Elijah when he was taken away, Elijah was not imparting the office, since Elisha already had it. Elijah obviously didn't have a double portion of his own anointing!

He was merely uttering a conditional prophecy from God that Elisha would receive more prophetic power, an even stronger ability to speak and interpret the Word of God.

I conclude from this that a prophet, for example, can pray an impartation of prophetic gifting (ability to hear from God and speak it forth more readily) but cannot confer or impart the office of prophet. An apostle, or anyone with leadership ability even if not an apostle, can do the same. In fact, as we have already discussed, part of "equipping" is for people gifted in the five-fold areas to train up others in them. Some may in fact attain one of the offices, but only if called to it by God.

A Simple Prayer of Impartation

As a model, here again is the simple prayer of impartation we used in Chapter 12:

"Lord, I thank you for the gifts you have given me, particularly the gift of _____, and I pray now that you would impart this gift to (Name)."

Then, addressing the person, "(Name), as God has gifted me

with _____ characteristics/talent/power, in Jesus' name I impart these to you by the power of the Holy Spirit. Freely I have received, now freely I give. Receive this impartation now, in the name of Jesus. Amen."

Feel free to vary this any way you like to fit the need or the circumstances.

ACTIVATION EXERCISES (YES, EVEN IN AN APPENDIX)

1. Does this discussion make you want to receive a greater impartation of one or more gifts and talents bestowed by God? Which ones? Why (very important)?

2. Pray and ask God which ones He would like you to have, or to have more of. Does your list line up with His answer? If so, ask Him for a direct impartation.

3. Make a list of people you know who are proficient in the gifts you've prayed about. If an appropriate opportunity arises (or you can create one), ask and see if these people would be willing to pray a prayer of impartation over you for whatever it is. If they don't know about this or have trouble believing they can do it, explain to them what you've learned about it in this book, including the Bible references.

4. Can you think of anyone you would like to bless by imparting something you have?

ABOUT THE AUTHOR

Walt Pilcher is a former CEO of Kayser-Roth Corporation, L'eggs Products division of Sara Lee Corporation, and Nihon Sara Lee, KK (Japan). He holds a BA from Wesleyan University and an MBA from Stanford University. He has been a church elder and served on the Board of Trustees of Regent University, the Board of Directors of The United Way of Greater Greensboro, and the Business School Advisory Board at Greensboro College. Walt currently serves on the Board of Directors of The Apostolic Network of Global Awakening, an international Christian evangelistic ministry. He was an editor of *In-Store Marketing: A New Dimension in the Share Wars* by Michael Wahl and *More than We Can Imagine: A Practical Guide to the Holy Spirit* by Rev. Dick Robinson, and he has published a number of articles, short stories and poems. Walt and his wife, Carol, an artist, have three children and six grandchildren. They live in Greensboro, North Carolina, and attend Grace Church in High Point, North Carolina.

"One of the greatest rewards in my career has been seeing people grow and mature personally, professionally, and spiritually and to feel that maybe I contributed in some way," he says. "I pray *The Five-fold Effect* can help others do the same in their own work and lives."